Menace in the West

Colorado and the American
Experience with Drugs, 1873-1963

MENACE

IN THE WEST

Colorado and the American
Experience with Drugs,
1873-1963

by Henry O. Whiteside

COLORADO HISTORICAL SOCIETY

Office of Research and Publications
David N. Wetzel, Publications Director
David Fridtjof Halaas, Chief Historian

Menace in the West
Editor, Steven G. Grinstead
Designer, Laetitia Lawler

Library of Congress Cataloging-in-Publication Data

Whiteside, Henry O., 1942–
    Menace in the West : Colorado and the American experience with
drugs, 1873-1963 / by Henry O. Whiteside.
        p.   cm.
    Includes index.
    ISBN 0-942576-38-1
    1. Drug abuse—Social aspects—Colorado—History. 2. Drug abuse—
Government policy—Colorado—History. 3. Narcotics, Control of—
Colorado—History. 4. United States. Bureau of Narcotics.
    5. Narcotic laws—United States.   I. Title.
HV5831.C6W48 1997
362.29'09788—dc21
                                                                97–9940

CONTENTS

Cover: Clerks stand ready to help the day's customers in Denver's A. G. Clark Drug Store, 1900–1910.

Chapter 1 appeared in similar form as "The Drug Habit in Nineteenth-Century Colorado" in *The Colorado Magazine* 55 (winter 1978), 46–68.

For my mother, who wanted me to write.

About the author
Several years ago, the publication of a definitive work abruptly changed
the author's plans to spend a sabbatical from Colorado Women's College
researching the origins of the federal Marijuana Tax Act of 1937. He
turned instead to the material at hand—Colorado's own experience with
drugs. He is currently director of development for the Utah Opera.

Preface

N ALMOST every time and culture, psychoactive substances have been both widely used and banned or restricted. Through the eighteenth century, Americans primarily restricted the use of alcohol and, to a much lesser extent, tobacco. The reforming temper of the 1830s and 1840s, however, produced a widespread effort to eliminate their use altogether. The belief in reason and the possibility of progress that invigorated these crusades also underlay the contemporary outward thrust of both European science and empire. Empire-building Europeans encountered numerous psychoactive substances long used by other cultures. At the same time, the pioneers of modern pharmacology were learning to isolate and refine the active principles of traditional drugs, to synthesize their principles, and to create still more. As the territory of Colorado approached statehood, the first fruits of these discoveries—primarily abundant and inexpensive preparations of opium—had already found an unobtrusive place in American life.

Three generations later a striking transformation had taken place. The hopeful products of nineteenth-century science had supplanted alcohol and tobacco as social menaces. Americans had come to see a major threat in the nonmedical use of drugs, in "dope." By the early 1950s the features of this new menace had been thoroughly discerned. Geographic location, diverse ethnic heritage, and rapid economic development insured that Coloradans experienced this progression with a broader range of drugs than did the citizens of most other states. And yet Colorado provides a more representative case study of the American experience with drugs than the coastal states, dominated by the experience of their heavily affected port cities.

Since the nineteenth century, investigators have lamented the difficulty of assessing the actual prevalence of illicit drug use. Contemporary indicators of the extent of drug use will therefore be introduced chiefly to cast light on popular attitudes. We will consider here Coloradans' evolving perception of a menace in drugs and their attempts to counter it. In the light of their experience, little of our contemporary drug problem seems truly new.

I would like to express my gratitude to the librarians of the major collections I consulted: the Denver Public Library's Western History Department and the Colorado Historical Society in Denver, and the federal Drug Enforcement Administration and the American Pharmaceutical Association, both in Washington, D.C. I am indebted for critical reading and advice to Thomas J. Noel, University of Colorado at Denver, Alan Culpin, and Floyd A. O'Neil, director of the American West Center at the University of Utah; for prodding to Wallace S. Brooke, M.D., and my father, Henry O. Whiteside; and for meticulous editing to Steve Grinstead of the Colorado Historical Society. The Von Otterberg Institute extended patient support for preparation of the manuscript.

Mechling and Shallcross store at Fourteenth and Larimer Streets in Denver, 1870–79. Denver Public Library, Western History Department.

Chapter One

Drugs of Habit in Nineteenth-Century Colorado

OLORADANS of the 1870s knew the medical use of perhaps a dozen psychoactive drugs. Physicians, lacking effective medications and knowing little of the physiological bases of disease, could at best only relieve symptoms. Opiates, as they had from ancient times, stood head and shoulders above other agents of relief. Opium relieved pain, induced sleep, reduced muscle spasm, checked diarrhea, and indeed seemed a panacea. The traditional name for an alcoholic tincture of opium, *laudanum*, reflected its stature—"to be praised."[1]

In 1807 chemists isolated morphine, the active principle of opium, beginning a remarkable series of discoveries that expanded the traditional store of plant-derived drugs. By mid-century ether, chloroform, and chloral hydrate had armed the surgeon with general anesthetics. By the 1880s bromides had begun to replace traditional sedatives. Aspirin provided both a mild painkiller and a fever reducer. In 1884 cocaine was demonstrated as the first topical anesthetic.

In Colorado's early years, medicine itself was making a difficult transformation into a unified profession. Practitioners of radically differing schools assailed each other as quacks as readily as they awarded themselves the title of "doctor." As towns flourished and died overnight, doctors were few and "as roving as their patients."[2] Treatment was often self-prescribed and drew upon home medical guides, widely advertised patent medicines, or the advice of the local pharmacist or merchant who sold medicines. Residents of remote mining camps and isolated farmsteads faced ailments from toothache to typhoid fever and the constant risk of injury. Most armed themselves with cure-all patent medicines dependent on opium.[3]

Medical men understood that opium was addicting. By the 1870s addiction was well described in medical texts and reference books.[4] Hope persisted, however, that addiction could be averted by chemical modification or some new means of delivery, such as hypodermic injection, introduced in the 1850s. Addiction was unfortunate, but a secondary consideration. Indeed, opium was widely employed despite general knowledge of a far more serious defect—its potential as a lethal poison. Too strong a dose stopped breath and life. Opiates and other psychoactive drugs were in fact first regulated not as agents of addiction but as potential poisons.

Laymen too were surely aware in a general sense of the danger of addiction. Home medical guides listed opiates as both likely poisons and as antidotes suitable for use against other poisons. Addiction was often dealt with as "chronic opium poisoning."[5] Both suicides and murderers employed opiates, and fatal overdoses of patent medicines—their contents unknown or misjudged—were common. Physicians repeatedly warned that thousands of children had died from the opium in remedies like Mrs. Winslow's Soothing Syrup. The Colorado Territorial Legislature acted in 1872 to regulate the sale of poisons, and Denver's Charter and Ordinances of 1875 made sale of unmarked poisons a misdemeanor punishable by a fine of up to $100. Both presumably applied to pure opiates, but neither controlled patent medicines laced with opium. An act of the Colorado Legislature of 1885 "Regulating the Practice of Pharmacy and the sale of medicines and poisons" explicitly included opiates and imposed comparable penalties. By comparison, legislation regulating the sale and consumption of alcohol was both more frequent and more complex.[6]

Opium Smoking, an Alien Vice

Coloradans never extended their easy acceptance of medicinal opium to the smoking of opium. Opium smoking, encountered in the China trade, was soon viewed as a vice, more readily so because monarchist Great Britain encouraged it. Chinese laborers, initially imported for railroad construction, were by the 1870s increasingly common in Colorado mining camps. Coloradans displayed both contempt and bemused curiosity at the peculiar ways of the "Celestials," including their smoking of opium.

The editor of the weekly *Central City Register* described them as "a quiet, inoffensive class" to whom the American "feast of liberty" should be fully open, "so long as they conform to our laws." He denounced attempts to stir up hatred of the Chinese as the work of ambitious demagogues. More typical of late 1870s sentiment was an article captioned "The Opium Pipe: The Heathen Chinee and the Narcotic of Death; How John Smokes His Pipe."[7] Exposés of the opium dens or "hop joints" of Denver's Chinatown on lower Wazee Street were a periodic feature of the local press. Newspaper accounts worked the association of opium smoking with the Chinese to the mutual discredit of both.

Eventually Denver discovered that the unthinkable had begun to happen—whites, even women, girls, and boys, had begun "hitting the pipe." The *Denver Rocky Mountain News* applauded Leadville's simple elimination of the opium threat by driving out the Chinese.[8] In the summer of 1880, as the national elections approached, "the Chinese question" was stridently agitated in Colorado. Attacks on the unfair competition of cheap Chinese labor and their repellent vice of opium smoking increased in frequency and virulence. Nationally, the Democrats capitalized on this resentment by publishing the "Morely Letter," purporting to show President Garfield's support of unrestricted immigration.

As agitation against Denver's Chinese mounted, the death of an eighteen-year-old boy prompted the first general raid on the dens. The city coroner determined that the boy's death on October 8, 1880, had been caused by typhoid and a perforated intestine, his symptoms masked by medicinal opium. The coroner's jury, however, reported that the death had been caused immediately by a perforated intestine and remotely by an "excessive use of opium." The *Denver Tribune* was Republican, sympathetic to business interests, and not eager to ban cheap Chinese labor, but nevertheless captioned its account "The Deadly Drug: A Young Man of Denver Falls Victim to the Prevailing Chinese Vice." The *Rocky Mountain News*, adamantly Democratic and violently anti-Chinese, headlined the story "Deadly Opium—Kills a Lad Eighteen Years of Age" and raged against the dens "in the very heart of the city." The *News* concluded that it was "high time some measures were taken to wipe out one of the foulest blots on modern civilization."[9]

The *News* readily took credit for rousing the community to press police for the subsequent raid on the dens. The trial, described as "an unusual spectacle," brought fines for four Chinese and two whites. Others escaped punishment, "as the law requires that they should be detected in the act of selling or smoking opium to sustain an offense." Whether the judge proceeded upon the ordinance prohibiting disorderly houses or upon an ordinance specifically directed against "opium joints" is unclear. An officer reportedly declared that smoking opium was illegal, but no such ordinance has been found.[10]

The dens' proprietors quickly recovered from the raid, viewing the fines as a kind of occupational tax. The *News*, critical of lax enforcement, found "some truth" in this view and continued its campaign against the Chinese. A headline warned that it was a case of "Caucasian against Mongolian—the Survival of the Fittest." Next day the editors had glorious news: "Chinese Gone! Chinatown Now a Mass of Ruins, The Opium Dens Razed to the Ground by an Enraged and Infuriated Populace." A mob had descended on Chinatown, Sixteenth Street between Blake and Wazee, ransacked it, put its two hundred some residents to flight, and beaten an elderly Chinese man to death. Denver's political factions abused each other as "Democratic demagogues" and "radical Republicans" and traded accusations of having incited the riot for partisan advantage, but the *News* staunchly defended destruction of the opium and prostitution dens.[11]

The riot and the passing of the national election drew much of the heat from discussion of both Chinese immigration and opium. Denver's first known ordinance against maintaining or patronizing opium joints passed during this period of comparative calm. The doubly ironic sequel was the arrest of a white man for allowing Chinese to smoke in his room after the October riot. "This is the first case of this character," commented the *News*, "and the sticking qualities of the ordinance will be tested." But so diminished was the sense of urgency that an overworked clerk had not yet properly recorded and certified the ordinance, and the case was dismissed.[12]

The penalties of $50 to $300—though stiff compared to $5 to $100 for maintaining a bawdy house or $25 to $100 for assisting a jail break— had not prevented the reopening of many dens. Significantly, the Chinese believed that they had been fined for selling to whites, and the *News* seemed reassured that "no opium is now being sold to Americans." But by January 6, 1881, three white women had been arrested for smoking opium. The discovery that "pulling" a joint did not close it permanently led city authorities to reaffirm their intention of closing the opium dens for good. They also warned that "in the future, all white persons caught in the opium pits will be prosecuted just as rigorously as the Chinese." Nevertheless, press attention to raids in Denver and mining towns such as Georgetown and Fairplay soon became desultory, and judges assessed penalties far milder than the maximums. The *News* eventually published a lengthy piece deflating the opium menace as greatly overstated and "considerably lied about."[13]

This first "dope" scare prefigured subsequent episodes of public concern with the menace of drugs. The press brought to public attention the private, even secret, behavior of drug users, of which the vast majority of Denver citizens could hardly otherwise have been aware. The drug menace was readily manipulated for partisan advantage, particularly when plied in conjunction with racial fears. The fear of drugs was easily aroused, but just as easily placated by the enactment of stiff penalties. Subsequent enforcement might be lax or nonexistent, but public interest readily returned to more present and immediate concerns.

Perceptions of Drug Use

While Denver's interest in opium smoking waned, national concern with drug habits was rising. In the 1870s the danger of opiates, particularly the delusive reliance on injection to escape addiction, had been dealt with primarily in medical literature.[14] By the 1880s discussions of drug use were often directed to laymen. Dr. George Beard's *American Nervousness: Its Causes and Consequences* traced heavy drug use to the rapid pace of modern life, which required "soothing." Beard had extended the contemporary argument that Americans in particular were prone to rely on drugs of all kinds. Studies revealing the surprising extent of opium use in rural areas as well as cities fueled public concern.[15]

Coloradans believed that the habitual use of drugs involved every element of society, from the unknowing to the willfully addicted. Opiates were the primary drugs of habit, but users of chloral hydrate, chloroform, ether, the bromides, and other sedatives and hypnotics also grew dependent. Introduction to opiates under a doctor's care and the profusion of opiated patent medicines were equally blamed for addiction. Certainly those addicted by patent medicines, particularly children habituated to soothing syrups and teething remedies, were considered the most hapless victims. A Colorado physician sketched the common sequence: "The many nostrums on the market such as cough syrups, throat ease, and bowel mixtures have started a craving for some narcotic which the patient learns sooner or later that morphine alone satisfies."[16] Although doctors prescribing opiates were admonished not to tell the patient, once the relief of opium had been experienced, discovery of the source could hardly have been difficult. The most common route to involuntary addiction seems to have been self-administration, following the conventional wisdom of friends or a remembered prescription.

Potent drugs, most often opiates, might be obtained on request in pure form, in standard preparations such as laudanum or paregoric, or in "catch penny products, put upon the market by persons of business enterprise and without an excess of scrupulousness and wafted into a certain vogue—temporary and inglorious . . . as a remedy that, in the hands of some physician in a distant country, has, according to the early published reports that reach us, produced wonderful results in the cure or mitigation of some disease . . . ."[17] Many of these preparations were called "tonics," "cordials," or "elixirs" and were intended not so much to cure a particular disease or diseases as simply to promote a general feeling of health and well-being. Most, like Godfrey's Cordial, relied on a fruit syrup, alcohol, and a liberal dose of opium. By the late 1880s patent medicine men had discovered a new drug ideally suited to their tonics. Cocaine soon made its appearance in such products as Vin Mariani and Wyeth's Wine of Coca.[18]

In the fall of 1884 an American physician returning from an Austrian medical convention had reported cocaine as the first effective topical anesthetic, insuring its widespread and rapid introduction in the United States. The following spring a Denver newspaper noted the use of "cocaine, the new and valuable anesthetic."[19] The drug's exhilarating properties were quickly recognized. Cocaine was soon available not only in a variety of medical preparations, but also as a simple powder under sug-

Popular tonics and cordials often achieved their desired effects through liberal doses of opium or cocaine. These women are relaxing at Denver's White and McMahan drugstore at Twenty-first and Larimer; a sign above the counter advertises a brand of "strengthening cordial." Denver Public Library, Western History Department.

gestive names like "Bright Eye." Bars served it by the pinch in a shot of whisky, and popular tonics like Koka-Nola, Celery Kola, and the candidly named Coca-Cola relied on it. An 1890s poster promoting Coca-Cola as the smart after-theater drink promised "it relieves fatigue and excitement, and induces a spirit of thorough, restful satisfaction as delightful to the senses as Coca-Cola is to the sense of taste."[20]

The demand for tonics and cordials reflected a category of drug users intermediate between unknowing medical addicts and those addicted in the simple pursuit of pleasure. Ambitious and hard-working men—including doctors, lawyers, and even ministers—used drugs to overcome fatigue and then to bring sleep. But among "opium eaters" or drinkers, women were believed to outnumber men by a margin of greater than ten to one. A Colorado physician observed:

> Opium eating is the growing and fashionable vice among the rich—
> especially the fashionable women, who, in the giddy round of eva-
> nescent pleasure, must have stimulants. Whiskey and champagne
> are painful in their after effects rather than pleasant. Beer is vulgar
> and it fattens, and no fashionable lady wants to be fat. Hence opium
> is resorted to. It can be taken without exciting the gossip that a free
> use of Heidsick [champagne] might bring about. You can get it in
> the drugstore in the shape of Munn's Elixir.

Women were considered more likely to depend on opium because "they
are naturally more nervous than men and feel the need for something to
soothe them." The same writer suggested that the perverse effect of strong
temperance sentiment was that women "fearful of names rather than
consequences give themselves over to the use of opiates." "Men," observed
another writer, "can find consolation in the flowing bowl of bad whiskey
which is very cheap in Denver . . . ." "Between the opium den of the
Chinese and its quiet consumption by Caucasians," he concluded, "Denver is getting up a reputation as quite a good market for the drug."[21]

The more affluent, with their readier access to medical attention, were
believed to become addicted by injecting morphine. The more usual progression was thought to begin with consuming opium in some palatable
preparation, then to progress to eating the raw drug, and finally to injection. Few doubted that opium was widely used at the lower end of the
social scale. Opium smoking among the Chinese was accorded a con-
temptuous tolerance and recognized with regret among white gamblers,
criminals, and prostitutes. Press reports of raids on opium joints carefully enumerated Chinese and whites, males and females, usually including several white women, often identified as "sporting women."

A Qualified Acceptance of Drug Use
Nevertheless, medical opinion did not sharply differentiate opiate addiction from other drug habits. A home medical manual characteristically
warned against "the evils of habitually exciting the nerves by the use of
tobacco, opium, narcotics and other drugs." A full page on the dangers of
tobacco closed with the brief warning that the "opium habit . . . is open to
the same objections." Indeed, "narcotic" described anything that could
produce stupor or a semi-comatose state, including alcohol, chloral hy-

drate, the bromides, and even illuminating gas. A standard reference work remarked that "every race and tribe is possessed of some stimulant in its armamentarium of life." The manual mentioned alcohol, tea, coffee, and coca leaves and referred casually to "a man addicted to the use of coffee." In discussing alcohol another authority referred to "a natural desire for stimulants and narcotics which seems to be common to all mankind but which, fortunately, the vast majority of men, at least, are able to control."[22]

The popular press reflected this qualified philosophical acceptance of the use of stimulants, exhilarants, alcohol, and opiates. "The unnatural vices of any kind," a reporter observed, "are quite apt to be overcome in some way or another or outgrown, and the world at large is probably less liable to go to the devil in this year of grace 1885 than it was a couple of centuries ago." He concluded that

... knowledge, however widespread, never seems likely to deprive the fool killer of his vocation. As long as the world is as it is and people work for small salaries, a certain percentage of humanity will drink more cheap whiskey than is good for them, and a certain percentage of them will get beguiled by opium, chloral, and other deadly drugs. Physicians are pretty generally of the opinion that in this world of pain and suffering, disappointment and sorrow, a world where disease is more likely to baffle the physician than otherwise, opiates, narcotics, and anesthetics, wine, laudanum, morphine and chloral are among the most valued agents in certain cases.

For all that, he observed, few would advocate a steady diet of narcotics or go so far as to class alcohol and tobacco among them.[23]

The Women's Christian Temperance Union (WCTU) shared neither this philosophical tolerance, nor the lack of faith in education, nor the reluctance to class alcohol and tobacco as narcotics. A Vermont law of 1882 requiring schools to teach the effects of alcohol and narcotics became the model promoted by the WCTU in a nationwide campaign that eventually spanned more than thirty years. Ten states had adopted comparable laws before 1887, when the Colorado legislature passed a bill "To Provide for the Study of the Nature of Alcoholic Drinks and Narcotics and of their effects upon the Human System," Colorado's first law specifically directed against drug habits.[24]

The hand of the WCTU is also apparent in an 1898 Denver ordinance requiring cigarette dealers to present an affidavit of good character, a $500 bond, and an annual license fee of $1,000. A liquor license, by comparison, could be obtained for a fee of $600. The Denver cigarette ordinance carefully denied any intent to authorize the "sale of cigarettes containing opium, chloral, morphine, jimpson weed, belladonna, glycerine or sugar."[25] Because reformers feared that the mildness and convenience of cigarettes would spread the use of tobacco to women and the young, they often asserted that cigarettes were commonly doctored with opium, *Cannabis indica*, and other narcotics. Nevertheless, Colorado did not join the fourteen states which at one time or another between 1895 and 1921 banned the sale of cigarettes altogether.[26]

Cures: A Gauge of Addiction

The most telling gauge of addiction in Colorado was the proliferation of cures. Patent remedies for the cure of addiction were heavily promoted, Colorado physicians experimented with cures in their own practices, private "institutes" flourished, and in 1893 Colorado became one of the first states to provide for cures at public expense. Cures were directed primarily against alcohol but were touted for addiction to other drugs and for "nervous disorders" as well.[27] The volume of advertisements for proprietary cures suggests the extent of unwanted addiction to alcohol, drugs, and even tobacco. Available by mail or from local pharmacists, remedies were often suggested for involuntary cure of "loved ones" to whom they might be given unawares in coffee or tea. Incredibly, these nostrums almost invariably relied on opium, morphine, or codeine for their "cures." One proprietor brazenly used the name of a preparation of opium traditional since the Middle Ages for his "Theriaki Painless Cure—Discovered in 1868—the only painless Cure ever discovered."[28]

A study by the state analyst of Massachusetts of twenty of the nation's most widely advertised cures found that all but one contained morphine. The exception touted "a double chloride of gold," but contained none. Ineffective as they were, the "gold cures" were preferable to the standard cures, in all of which a Colorado physician found opiates. Gold had enjoyed a revival early in the nineteenth century in the hands of the "auralists," who preferred it to mercury in their treatment of syphilis. In the 1880s gold returned to popular favor in medicines. Compounded with chlorine, bromine, iodine, arsenic, and mercury in such concoctions as Dr. Haines' Golden Specific, gold was briefly in vogue in cures for addiction.[29]

A host of private institutes sprang up across the nation to accommodate those desperate for cures and able to afford a course of treatment as inpatients. Some of these appear to have been enterprises of physicians who believed they had developed an effective plan of treatment. A Wyoming doctor, for example, convinced that the cure lay in iodine, scouted other physicians for a commercial venture expected to be quite profitable. The institutes all advertised their association with a "doctor" or with a famous cure, such as the German Cure or the Bellevue Hospital Cure. Colorado's climate exerted so great an attraction that by the 1880s a state official believed as many as one-third of the state's residents might have been characterized as "health seekers."[30] Consequently, many purveyors of cures chose to locate in Colorado, primarily in Denver but also in Pueblo, Colorado Springs, and Glenwood Springs.

Foremost among these were the local establishments in the national chain of Keeley Institutes, among the earliest commercial cures in Denver and the last to disappear. Provision for cures at public expense in 1893 led to a temporary increase in the number of institutes, including one sponsored by Pastor Tom Uzzell to provide "real care," rather than to shuffle clients in and out for medication. Keeley was followed by other national enterprises, such as Dr. Pettey's Retreats, and independent ventures like Woodcroft in Pueblo and Forest Retreat in Denver.[31] The institutes typically promised rapid, complete, and permanent cures, solicitous care, and discretion.

The regimens these institutes offered did not differ greatly in principle from treatment offered by Colorado physicians in private practice. Colorado's doctors, defensive perhaps about any suggestion of rough-edged frontier medicine, were surprisingly active in professional organizations. The editor of *Colorado Medicine*, journal of the state medical society, estimated that more than half the members of county societies regularly received the *Journal of the American Medical Association*, although as yet the association only aspired to speak for the profession. In 1903, 60.2 percent of Colorado's physicians—nearly twice the national average—responded to the American Pharmaceutical Association's survey of addiction. Not surprisingly, then, their treatments were usually variations on treatments described in contemporary professional literature.[32]

Treatments for alcoholism, morphinism, and cocainism—in that order the most frequently encountered addictions or "chronic poisoning"—were essentially similar. Withdrawal from the drug, usually rapid rather than abrupt or gradual, supportive therapy, and sedation and the easing of distress with hyoscine or atropine were expected to accomplish a physical cure within two to four weeks. Mild or violent purging at the outset was added as a standard feature of cures for opiate addiction, as was confinement to prevent access to the drug. Some believed the drugs themselves destroyed will power that could only be rebuilt over many months, if at all. Others traced the acquisition of the habit to an innately weak or self-indulgent nature. All agreed that a permanent cure depended ultimately on the patient's moral strength and will. Many considered permanent cures extremely unlikely.[33]

Although Colorado followed national trends in therapy, the state was among the first to provide for treatment at public expense for those habituated beyond their control. An act of 1893 allowed friends or kin to petition county commissioners to send "habitual drunkards" to "any reputable gold cure institute" at the county's expense. The petitioners were required to state that the drunkard had agreed to his treatment and that neither he nor his family could pay for a cure. They were further required to include the names of three reputable taxpayers who would attest to the appropriateness of county assistance. A final section extended the definition of "drunkard" to include "a person who has acquired the habit of using morphine, opium, or other narcotics to such a degree as to deprive himself of reasonable self-control."[34]

The Colorado legislature's preferment of gold cure institutes in the early years of the great Cripple Creek gold boom, while understandable, was nevertheless unfortunate. A medical inquiry into gold cures found that gold played an inconsequential part in a course of treatment dependent on injections of strychnine and atropine which, "administered several times daily for weeks, have been followed in a large number of cases by insanity and other serious psychoses." The counties, however, balked at accepting the cost of cures, gold or otherwise. The director of the Colorado Insane Asylum complained that the counties regularly dumped upon the asylum "Epileptics, imbeciles, and idiots, likewise drunkards or cases of alcoholism, morphine and cocaine habitués." "Paupers and other help-less subjects that might otherwise be cared for" were shunted to the asy-lum as well.[35]

A significant number of petitions must have been presented, because two years later a new statute repealed the act of 1893. The preferment of gold cure institutes was dropped, and institutions wishing to qualify were required to show that at least seventy-five percent of their patients remained cured for at least a year. Ten, rather than three, freeholders of the county were now required to approve the petition. A further revision in 1911 disallowed payment if an agent of the institute had been in-volved in procuring treatment and capped total payments under the fee schedule previously adopted. Because these three acts provided for treat-ment of alcoholism as well as drug addiction, they are uncertain indica-tors of public concern about drug habits. Note that treatment at public expense could only be extended to a person addicted "to such a degree as to deprive himself of reasonable self-control." Social irresponsibility rather than the fact of addiction was the determining factor, as it was in the commitment of the insane.[36]

Concern and Ambivalence in Controlling Dope
Neither was legislation restricting the sale of a drug a reliable gauge of public concern. Colorado restricted the sale of cocaine in 1897, following the example of Oregon in 1887 and Montana in 1889. The lack of opposi-tion might equally have reflected disinterest or concern. Social tensions ran high in 1890s Colorado. The collapse of silver prices protracted the national economic crisis of 1893, and problems of industrial growth, min-ing regulation, and railroads preoccupied the state legislature. Labor violence approaching industrial warfare was common throughout the decade. After its introduction in 1884, cocaine had rapidly acquired a diverse following. Criminals and prostitutes indulged in it, the ambi-tious and socially prominent used it to "brighten up," and laborers used it to fight off fatigue. Cocaine was initially sold in the commissaries of many Colorado mining camps, but quickly gained a reputation for caus-ing violence and insanity. Colorado's act of 1897 made it the third state

13

to require a prescription for the sale of cocaine. The origin of the bill, introduced by request from isolated La Plata County, a center of mining activity, may reflect both heavy use among miners and the tensions of labor unrest. Certainly the maximum fine of $300 was a stiff penalty.[37]

Denver Ordinance Number 75 of 1898 banning the "selling, exchanging, bartering, dispensing, and giving away of morphine, opium, and cocaine" without a prescription from "a reputable physician" set a penalty of $25 to $100. Introduced late in May, the bill passed shortly after the *Denver Times* captioned a story "Denver Makes No Effort to Check the Disease of Morphine and Opium Eating."[38] Cocaine, however, appears to have been added as an afterthought, the word written in on the printed copy of the bill preserved in the city vaults. The addition may reflect a last-minute judgment against relying on enforcement of the previous year's state cocaine law.

Neither that law nor the city ordinance seems to have been the product of urgent public concern or to have had any immediate consequences in practice. Strict laws were passed but enforced only sporadically. Six years after Denver's anti-Chinese riot and the passage of an ordinance carrying stiff fines, the writer of an opium exposé observed: "There are stringent municipal laws against [opium joints] but the laws are never enforced, and the majority of the people go on in blissful ignorance of their existence unless one happens to be raided. Then there is some talk about it which soon ceases. The fiends get over their fear and go on 'hitting the pipe' with their old-time recklessness." So indifferent does Denver appear to have been in its dealings with the opium joints that in the city code of 1886 a second ordinance appears in Section 28, separate from the ordinance of 1880 in Section 11 and essentially duplicating it, but with penalties ranging from $5 to $50 instead of $50 to $300.[39]

Despite the legislation of the 1890s and the occasional "outrage" stories in the press, there is ample evidence of relative public and official indifference to drugs. The press might report that the opium habit had grown in Denver and even spread to society women of Denver's "400," but the "hop fiends" fined after occasional raids on the dens typically paid modest fines of only $10 for patrons and $50 for proprietors. Smoking opium was still imported legally upon payment of a modest duty. Indeed, the Chinese in Denver provided a dependable market for smuggled opium confiscated by federal authorities and sold at public auction on the courthouse steps. Even less comprehensible were the plans of some of Denver's Chinese to open a Chinese-style hotel, "a sort of club where they can go and smoke opium in peace," "A New Chinese Hotel for Lovers of the Dope."[40] Despite laws against keeping a "den" or selling opium without a prescription, denying opium to whites seemed to present a particular difficulty.

Doctor A. L. Bennett, appointed state "Medical Inspector to Chinese" in 1901, believed that of the 1,100 Chinese in the state, Denver's colony of 400 was much more given to the opium vice than the colonies in Colorado Springs and Colorado City. He besieged the State Board of Health with requests that "some strict state law be enacted which can be enforced prohibiting the sale of opium to whites." He argued to no effect that the spread of opium smoking among whites in Denver, particularly young men and women, made legal action imperative. It should be a misdemeanor, he pleaded, "for a Chinese to permit whites to smoke opium in his den, or for white persons to be caught in the act of smoking opium."[41] Clearly, existing laws were not meant to apply to whites.

The comparative unconcern with drugs was also evident in the indifference to efforts by the State Board of Health to enforce the control of poisons. The board successfully enlisted the Denver Pharmaceutical Association's aid in condemning the sale of "B____'s ____ Powder" after its use addicted customers to cocaine. Aware of the limits to voluntary compliance, the board had then asked the state attorney general to clarify its power to require a list of contents on the label of proprietary drugs, confident that the new law of 1893 covered the problem "with fair thoroughness." The attorney general's reply was unsatisfactory, however, and the board concluded acidly that "it unfortunately appears to the technical mind that the law is not definite enough to answer the demands made upon it."[42]

In 1902, with the state law of 1897 restricting cocaine and the city ordinance of 1898 restricting opium, morphine, and cocaine several years on the books, the situation was unchanged. A Denver druggist described the usual practice to a coroner's jury investigating a woman's morphine suicide:

"We usually enter sales of poisons on the record, but not always in the case of confirmed morphine fiends. There are a great many people in the lower section of the city whom we know as regular fiends and we sell [to] them without making a record." Asked if that were not illegal he replied, rather doubtfully, "I suppose it is, but it would make a large record if we entered each sale, as many of them are small amounts."

A dime bought from one to five grains, depending on whether the purchaser was a regular customer; there was no fixed price. The coroner concluded that "the negligence in this respect is due, I think, to the fact that no prosecutions have ever been made for this offense."[43] Nor were Denver and Colorado unique for their laxness in controlling narcotics sales. A contemporary report of the American Pharmaceutical Association on the drug habit insisted on the need "to stop this sale of five and ten cents worth at a time—this running into a drug store and getting a few cents worth of a narcotic."[44]

Public perceptions of drug problems in nineteenth-century Colorado are not easily characterized. Strict laws were enacted and subsequently ignored. Coloradans saw habitual drug use as evil but were apparently indifferent to efforts at control. They were certainly aware of the lethal and addicting effects of drugs. They did not, however, see in drugs a distinctive social menace, nor did they see in laws the proper response to every social ill. Although they denounced the unlabeled inclusion of addicting drugs in patent medicines, they continued to view addiction as a regrettable development incident to the necessary use of opiates in the treatment of greater ills. Habitual use of drugs might be viewed as a vice or, if involuntarily contracted, as a misfortune, but it was only one among many that afflicted the people of nineteenth-century Colorado.

Impoverishment, insanity, and death can hardly have been seen as the distinctive fruits of drug addiction. In the unregulated financial cycles of the late nineteenth century, economic hardship, scarcely relieved by charitable assistance, was commonplace. Of 1,908 cases admitted to the State Insane Asylum at Pueblo between 1887 and 1900, the "supposed cause" of insanity recorded was 207 for alcohol, 119 from syphilis, 48 from "sexual self-abuse," and 33 from "religious excitement"—all ahead of drug use, the supposed cause of only 27 admissions.[45] Even if all deaths reported as suicides by poison are attributed to addicting drugs, the number would still be but a fraction of the deaths reported as caused by alcohol. Typhoid, tuberculosis, influenza, and endemic enteric fevers kept mortality rates high. In early Colorado death was a familiar and immediate experience, rarely mediated by hospitalization. An early physician recalled that death might proceed from something as incidental as the infection of a minor wound received in opening a nut with a penknife or as violent as firearms. "Shootings were a nightly occurrence in Denver, often fatal," he recalled. "It afforded many opportunities for the treatment of gunshot wounds."[46]

Among lapses in personal morality, drug use could hardly have loomed large in the shadow of alcoholism, with which it was generally associated by reformers and legislators alike. Sadder than the demand for opiate-laden "cures" of addiction was "the host of advertisements of remedies for venereal diseases" and "drugs or methods well understood to be intended to produce abortion" that filled the newspapers.[47] Finally, the presence of addiction in all elements of society and the abundant opportunities for "innocent" addiction insured that habitual drug users were not seen as alien to society.

Much addiction of this period was, in fact, unobserved and secret. Despite the early image of the debilitated "opium wretch," Colorado's physicians were increasingly aware of the difficulty of diagnosing addiction. Even during a physical examination, diagnosis often depended on the discovery of needle scars or abscesses. Earlier physicians had even experimented with switching alcoholics to opiates because of the lower incidence of debilitating effects. One Colorado doctor published a regimen to minimize even these effects in addicts unable or unwilling to be cured.[48] Indeed, many of Colorado's drug users may best be considered as having contracted a shameful disease, difficult to cure but manageable by regular use of "dope," readily and cheaply available.

An unidentified Denver pharmacist's lab at the turn of the century.
Denver Public Library, Western History Department.

Chapter Two

The Reformers Turn to State Regulation

HE REFORMING temper apparent nationally in the 1880s and 1890s was evident in Colorado, especially Denver, in the early 1900s. Neither of the established parties championed public responses to the social ills brought by industrialization, urbanization, and staggeringly rapid growth. Profits from routinely corrupt practices nourished Denver's machine politics, and payoffs allowed the opium joints to operate with impunity. In the 1890s, however, opinion slowly turned against this casual disregard for morals and public safety. The newly established *Denver Post* practiced a popular journalism that forced the Denver press to abandon traditional partisanship and compete actively for readers. The great drawing power of sensationalism in a righteous cause cemented press support for reforms. In Colorado the pure food and drug crusade found ready allies in opponents of both alcohol and "dope."

In the early 1900s, the focus and tone of the press changed. In 1905 health commissioner W. H. Sharpley assailed cocaine and morphine as "the curse of Denver." "The greatest evil," he said, "is the loose and careless way in which Denver druggists sell cocaine and morphine to so-called 'dope' fiends." Sharpley had found that other cities, disenchanted with local laws and enforcement, wanted "state laws of such stringent nature that the traffic can be checked if not entirely eradicated." Drawing on his experience as a police surgeon among the "unfortunate classes of Market Street," Sharpley estimated "5,000 slaves to cocaine and morphine in Denver."[1] This combination of sensational estimates, belief in the efficacy of harsher laws, and appeal to a higher level of government became increasingly common.

To pharmacists' dismay, accounts of opiates as poisons now joined the customary reports of opium joints "pulled" in Denver, Colorado Springs, and mining towns like Cripple Creek.[2] Morphine, alone or in combination with alcohol, was the instrument in a rash of suicides and accidental deaths. A drunken young woman managed on her third attempt to buy morphine, which combined with the alcohol to kill her. When another "morphine suicide" followed the next day, the *Denver Times* reported that these were the seventh and eighth such deaths in two weeks.[3] Druggists were commonly criticized for disregarding or complying only nominally with legal requirements for labeling, record-keeping, and determining a proper intended use.

Professional Self-Reform

The Colorado Pharmacal Association's members, typical of the professionals and independent small businessmen found in the ranks of progressive reformers, resented the charge that they trafficked in human misery. Because a pharmacist who refused to sell could expect the drug user to "take his business elsewhere," collaborative action seemed the only recourse. Then, too, the pharmacists' own proposals would forestall legislation drafted by laymen less knowledgeable and less sympathetic. Because early legislation controlled legitimate drug sales, associations of pharmacists and pharmaceutical manufacturers were heavily involved in producing model laws. Model statutes produced by the American Pharmaceutical Association (APhA), with which the Colorado Pharmacal Association was affiliated, greatly influenced Colorado laws, in particular those regulating pharmacy and the sale of narcotics.

The first attempt at an accurate estimate of the number of addicts in Colorado may have heightened interest in legislation. In 1903 the APhA's Committee on the Acquirement of the Drug Habit reported that narcotics use was increasing. The three survey returns from Colorado reported a total of twenty-one known addicts: eleven men and ten women; twenty whites and one "colored"; three addicted to crude opium, three to tincture of opium (laudanum), eleven to morphine, and two to cocaine. These figures suggested to the committee a total of 1,811 addicts in Colorado. In Denver and the nation, morphine addiction appeared to equal addiction to all other opiates and cocaine combined. One Denver pharmacist reported that a "very stringent city ordinance in addition to the state law" had made it "if not impossible, quite difficult for the victim" to buy drugs.[4] The actual extent of drug use, however, necessarily remained debatable.

In 1906 Denver incorporated elements of the APhA's Model Anti-Narcotic Law of 1903 to extend and systematize the 1898 ordinance requiring prescriptions for the sale of poisons. The ordinance added strychnine, laudanum, and carbolic acid to morphine, opium, and cocaine as controlled substances and required that standardized prescription records be kept for official inspection. But Section 790, "False Statements and Improper Prescription by Physicians Forbidden," departed significantly from the ordinance of 1898 by forbidding physicians "to give away any such order or prescription for a dose or quantity greater than usual or necessary for bona fide purposes to cure or prevent sickness or disease." Section 790 was meant to drive out the "dope doctors from whom prescriptions might be obtained for $.50 prior to 6:00 PM, $.75 from 6:00 PM until 12:00, and thereafter for $1.50."[5]

The APhA's model code flatly prohibited furnishing or prescribing for "the use of any habitual user," but by allowing normal prescriptions for treatment in good faith, the Denver ordinance preserved the physician's right to treat addiction itself. The ordinance reflected an emerging view of addiction as a disease responsive to treatment rather than a "loathsome and degrading habit."[6] Seeking to make the model statute attractive for widespread adoption, the APhA had cautiously skirted this distinction. By its silence, the Colorado Medical Society confirmed that the law was understood to apply only to the "dope doctors." Even curbing "dope doctors," however, lacked apparent urgency. The ordinance provided only mild regulatory fines of $10 to $100 and no special penalties for sales to addicts.

The following year the Colorado legislature routinely revised controls of poisons, without any apparent concern for addictive drugs. Sales without a prescription required only a simple record of the purchaser's name and address, the substance sold, and "the purposes for which it is represented by the purchaser to be required." Sales with a prescription required no purchase record of any kind.[7] Two months later the legislature controlled poisonous and addicting drugs more directly. The Colorado Pure Food and Drug Act echoed the previous year's federal Pure Food and Drug Act. The Colorado statute was "the same as Federal Law" and explicitly fitted to it. Both acts forbade the adulteration of foods with a number of categories of substances, among which were narcotic drugs. The acts required the labeling on nonprescription remedies to indicate the content of alcohol, morphine, opium, cocaine, heroin, Alpha and Beta Eucaine, chloroform, *Cannabis indica*, chloral hydrate, and acetanilide. The list was unusually comprehensive and notable for its inclusion of cannabis—marijuana. These labeling requirements were aimed squarely at manufacturers of patent medicines that depended covertly on cocaine or opiates. In sharp contrast to the earlier state pharmacy act, violations were felonies. The State Board of Health soon reported that pharmacists, unlike manufacturers, had responded in a "highly commendable" way, condemning deceptive advertising and the sale of mislabeled products.[8]

The Reformers Target Dope
The scattered victories for reform in the late 1890s and early 1900s were followed by a quickening succession of achievements. Disgusted with the fraud and incompetence traditional in both the Democratic and Republican parties, voters first elected a "clean" governor in 1906, and then in 1908 and 1910 a capable champion of reform, John F. Shafroth. Denver had earlier opted for a local solution to the problem of corruption in the state legislature by winning a constitutional amendment granting the city "home rule." Merger into the City and County of Denver, approved at the same time, promised greater efficiency and economy, as did adoption of the commission system of municipal government. Unfortunately, the first mayor of the newly combined city and county, Robert W. Speer, found an unbeatable combination in enlightened civic improvements and unregenerate political methods.

In this atmosphere of civic advancement, the easy availability of "dope" was intolerable. The press readily allied itself with Denver officials alarmed by the estimate of "5,000 slaves of cocaine and morphine" in the city. "Dope" emerged as the subject of Sunday supplement features, clearly indicating growing public interest. While cautionary to the reader, the tone was still likely to be sympathetic to the "victim," as it was in a Sunday *News-Times* full-page, illustrated article captioned "Woman Struggling Against Morphine Warns Others." But the Market Street opium joints, vestiges of Denver's adolescence, had become unacceptable.[9]

Crusade against the Opium Dens

The sporadic "pulling" of opium joints slowly gave way to well-planned raids upon the whole of Hop Alley, intended not to milk the dens continually but to close them permanently. Federal Customs Service agents and the Secret Service, enforcing the import duties on smoking opium, often led combined raids with city police. The reforming impulse behind these raids was evident in a former China missionary's plans to organize a society of "educated" Chinese to drive out the joints. The effective solution, the missionary assured readers, would be a complete ban on importing smoking opium.[10]

Public Law No. 221, "An Act to Prohibit the Importation and Use of Opium for Other than Medicinal Purposes," was shortly passed by Congress in February of 1908. Its primary purpose was not, however, to end the use of opium in the United States. Officials of the United States Department of Agriculture (USDA), in fact, considered the act completely unnecessary. Section 11 of the Pure Food and Drug Act, administered by the USDA, already authorized barring imports of any dangerous drug. The State Department had insisted that excluding opium was not the point. Specific anti-opium legislation would demonstrate American sincerity in pressing for a treaty controlling the opium trade. Nor did Public Law 221 close the opium joints in Denver. For nearly half a century, legal imports of opium had fallen when import duties rose and increased when duties fell. The obvious inference, given the steady demand for opium, was that when duties rose and legal imports fell, smuggled opium made up the difference. The success of a raid in July of 1909 that found the dens prospering might have been explained by stocks of opium on hand. But two years later, Internal Revenue agents leading a raid concluded that the opium seized had recently come in from Mexico.[11]

Temperance Sentiment: Singling out Dope

The same reforming sentiments that closed the opium dens fueled the much more prominent campaign against alcohol. Alcohol's opponents were active in Colorado even in territorial days. In 1897 anti-alcohol crusaders abandoned their attempt to create a third party in favor of the nonpartisan Anti-Saloon League, which in 1907 successfully pressed the legislature to allow prohibition of alcohol at local option. Prior to this time neither reformers, medical men, nor legislators had drawn a sharp line between alcohol and drugs. The 1887 act promoted by the Women's Christian Temperance Union and the Prohibition Party had required instruction in the effects of both alcohol and narcotics. A state legislator called for a bill to punish "parents and dealers in narcotics and liquors whose children may secure tobacco, cigarettes, and liquors." A Public Health Service survey in 1903 included state laws "that tend to show that alcohol is recognized as both a poison and a narcotic." The survey found such laws in forty-seven states and territories, but not Colorado.[12]

The reformer's comprehensive definition in part was meant to blacken alcohol by associating it with narcotics, already tainted with a sinister reputation. But the anti-alcohol crusaders would have been compelled to attack dope in any case: their opponents charged that prohibition of alcohol would produce a huge increase in the use of drugs. Testimony on opium before a House committee, for example, included a typical charge that morphine use in the teetotaling states had increased by over fifty percent between 1900 and 1910.[13] Opposition to dope advanced readily in Colorado, along with efforts at statewide prohibition of alcohol—which was only narrowly defeated in 1912.

An Evolving Perception of a "Drug Problem"

In the early 1900s dope was emerging as a matter of national interest, although still a very secondary concern. President Taft's message to the Senate advocating adoption of the Hague Opium Convention of 1912 showed a more immediate concern than abolishing the opium habit in China. The president stressed the "startling fact" that opium importation had risen by 351 percent since 1860, while the population had increased by only 133 percent. Three-quarters of that opium was converted into morphine, of which more than eighty percent was consumed by "victims of the habit to their personal detriment and with appalling effects on general society." As much as 150,000 ounces of cocaine was illegitimately used annually "to make fiendish criminals of human beings." Finally, the president included tons of chloral and hypnotics among the drugs "consumed annually by the people of this country, who, it has been asserted, are rapidly becoming hopelessly addicted to the habitual use of narcotic drugs of various kinds."[14]

In 1911 a Weld County physician, Dr. Edwin K. Knowles, vividly characterized Colorado's drug use. Despite the Pure Food and Drug Act, patent medicines—especially opiate-laden "cures" for addiction—were still readily purchased at drug stores whose "proprietors would refuse to sell morphine or opium." The spreading use of narcotics he found undeniable, especially "among the educated classes." Women suffering pain from pelvic disorders often resorted to opiates; intellectual neurotics and vigorous men under stress might "seek relief from exhaustion by indulging in stimulants, first alcohol and later morphine." Many turned to narcotics for relief from alcoholic hangover or "just to get a good night's rest."

Knowles found a fundamental cause of drug use in the nature of contemporary American life. "The demand put upon the brain by modern life and by modern methods of living is too much for many of us. Horses are too slow; trains must travel ninety miles an hour or we will not take them . . . . We are living too fast . . . ." The worst of these drugs, however, "far worse than morphine, worse than opium, worse than alcohol, worse than hashish," was cocaine. "It destroys the moral sense, wrecks the mind and body. Cocaine is a crime producer. Police officers in the larger cities will tell you that the majority of crimes are committed while under the influence of a drug." His concern with cocaine reflected a rising fear of cocaine in Colorado.[15]

Cocaine: A Drug of Exceptional Menace

The Colorado legislature shared the national view of cocaine as a drug of exceptional menace. The model Anti-Narcotic Act adopted by the APhA in 1903 had grown out of an attempt to restrict cocaine. As Denver's health commissioner, W. H. Sharpley had earlier referred to cocaine as "the curse of Denver."[16] In 1911 as state senator and chairman of the Medical Affairs Committee, he proposed to replace the 1897 ban on the sale of cocaine without a prescription with stiffer controls on all cocaine transactions. Cocaine, whether sold or administered by physicians, would require detailed records. Selling or giving cocaine without a prescription, or offering to sell or give it, would all be prohibited. Fines of $200 to $350 and imprisonment in the county jail for up to six months were considerably stiffer than previous penalties of as little as $5 without provision for imprisonment. Sharpley's bill passed without opposition.[17]

Colorado joined many other states in closely restricting cocaine, widely regarded as a vice, but not opiates. The use of opiates to control pain was still considered an inescapable necessity and their abuse an unfortunate byproduct. The opium habit was now considered an intractable "disease" over which "the individual has little or no control." In contrast, the cocaine addict might be withdrawn "abruptly without danger of collapse or suffering." Consequently, cocaine use might be considered a willful vice, and no treatment would be needed for users whose supply might be dried up by the law.[18] Fear of violence associated with cocaine further explains its strict control in advance of other drugs of habit. Cocaine's reputation for fueling violence and superhuman strength eventually played an important part in turning public concern from what dope might do to the addict to what the addict might do to others.

Denver Deals with Addiction—as a Crime and a Disease

Belief that addiction warranted treatment and rehabilitation rose significantly prior to the First World War. Sympathy for addicts was evident in much of the public debate and legislation. The common use of cocaine by laborers in the decade of labor warfare climaxed by the Ludlow Massacre of 1914 might have been expected to, but apparently did not, tint public fear of the drug with anti-radical and anti-labor sentiment. Neither did the tide of new immigrants to Colorado mining towns from southern and eastern Europe link cocaine with foreigners. In sharp contrast, fear of cocaine-crazed blacks had become commonplace in the South and prompted adoption of the larger .38 caliber police revolver with its increased "stopping power." This connection apparently failed to appear in Colorado because, except for the Chinese, immigrants rarely brought drug habits with them.[19]

In February of 1912 Denver acted much more directly to limit non-medical use of and trafficking in both cocaine and the opiates. This revised ordinance was squarely aimed at addiction. Ordinance No. 20 replaced the 1906 ordinance regulating the sale of poisons with provisions regulating "the Selling, Furnishing, Giving Away, Obtaining and Procuring of Poisonous and Habit Forming Drugs." Improper obtaining was now subject to the same penalties as improper providing of drugs. Section 2 banned unrecorded prescribing or selling of a drug "to any person addicted to the habitual use" of that drug. Relatively liberal maximum strengths for exempt preparations such as cough remedies, paregoric, and cures for diarrhea and cholera secured the support of Denver pharmacists. Signed by Mayor Speer shortly before his defeat by a "clean" government coalition in March, the ordinance implemented the reform agenda without compromise.[20]

Concern for the addict was apparent in Denver's efforts to provide treatment as well as to enforce the new ordinance. Police commissioner George Creel, later Woodrow Wilson's publicist against the Germans, noted the "amazing prevalence of the drug habit" and insisted that it was "the city's duty to check the spread of the menacing vice and to relieve the torments of its victims who usually become dependents of the city sooner or later." Dr. Charles B. James, a former city and county physician, headed a major city effort to cure arrested "dope victims." On his first visit to the county jail's "dope ward," James examined eighteen men and twelve women.[21]

Viewing addiction as a disease, many physicians experimented in the hope of finding a successful cure. Cures such as the Lambert cure, first reported in 1909, were marketable and potentially lucrative. Popular sentiment was both more sympathetic to the addict and more hopeful of a cure than it had been or would become. A Colorado physician surveying contemporary treatments conveyed professional sentiment well: "These people are to be pitied, not censured. One might as well impute wrong to an individual who has fallen in front of a train. Such terms as 'Drug Fiend,' 'Dope Fiend,' are criminal. [These people] need tender, careful attention, psychical as well as physical."[22]

Denver health commissioner Dr. Oscar Hayes began efforts to curb the drug supply by enforcing the new and stringent restrictions applicable to druggists and physicians. But as legitimate sources dried up, the opium joints near Twentieth and Market Streets began to satisfy the demand for cocaine and morphine. Failing to interest the police, Commissioner Hayes mobilized his milk inspectors, meat-market checkers, and sanitary inspectors for a raid on Hop Alley in the spring of 1913. Years later, he recalled that the raid had "closed the dens for good." But a year after the raid, the *Denver Post* reported that Hop Alley's dives, closed for nearly a year, were now sufficiently prosperous to offer three "public" dens—two for whites, one for blacks. The price of smoking opium had increased to an unprecedented $70 for a 6-ounce can, presumably because of the act of 1909 banning imports. Opium smokers nevertheless reported that more opium was being smoked than ever before.[23]

Hayes turned his efforts to illicit drug dealers throughout the city. By fall he could report thirty-eight convictions of forty cases brought to trial. Press coverage of his efforts in the summer of 1914, amidst labor tensions and apprehensions of war in Europe, raised a brief dope scare. The *Rocky Mountain News* screamed, "21,000 Dope Slaves in Denver." It reported an extremely improbable estimate by the city health department that Denver was home to 9,000 habitual users of cocaine and 12,000 users of morphine and heroin. The article gave an unusually informative glimpse of enforcement patterns:

> Many of these habitual drug users come from the better families of the city, according to health officials, some from what is known as society, persons who live on Capitol Hill and obtain their drugs from obliging family physicians. Against this class the health department is helpless. It is against the class that frequents the lower parts of the city and gets its "dope" from unscrupulous physicians and druggists that efforts are now being centered. This is the class from which the crazed criminals come, the officials say.

A cooler report stressed that, although Capitol Hill contributed a minority of Denver's addicts, drugs held a particular appeal for "the younger generation of society." Denver police estimated the number of morphine and cocaine addicts in Denver at something over five hundred, half of whom were women. Opium smokers were believed to number about one hundred fifty, a third of them women.[24]

Creating the Illicit Drug Trade

Denver prohibited nonmedical use of habit-sustaining drugs before either the state or Congress did so, and the city's experience warrants assessment. Though the price of smoking opium increased tenfold in the five years after the 1909 importation ban, Denver's opium joints survived repeated attempts to shut down the Alley. The joints eventually disappeared—not because opiate use had declined, but because the forms of opium consumed, the types of users, and the places of use had changed. The dens had never been essential to the smoking of opium. One user reported opium "in every boarding house in Denver."[25] Restrictions on the import and use of smoking opium probably did contribute to the dens' decline by increasing the attractiveness of morphine—smuggled more profitably and used with no revealing odor. Closing the dens further dispersed the consumption of opiates throughout the city.

Comparably, eliminating pharmacists' sales to users created a new group of more mobile entrepreneurs. They were increasingly well organized, but not into professional associations with codes of good practice. Prior to Denver's enforcement campaign, the "usual way for a dope fiend to get drugs" was to buy a prescription from a "dope doctor." Thirty grains of morphine, a frequently cited estimate of a day's supply, cost about $.75. An addict might supply himself for as little as $1.25 a day, prescription cost included, and thereby provide a handsome unearned income to the city's less ethical pharmacists and physicians.[26] As police had anticipated, the success of the enforcement drive against pharmacists raised street prices. Higher prices inevitably attracted those with little income and few prospects to selling drugs. These new black market entrepreneurs readily supplied the demand previously filled by pharmacists' gray market sales.

Finally, enforcement against poorer users who relied on prescription mills of dope doctors drew the most press attention. The affluent addict could receive treatment or maintenance from the family physician, sheltered by the confidentiality of a professional relationship. Continuing publicity about enforcement against "the class from which the crazed criminals come" slowly reinforced the association of dope with the lower classes and, above all, with criminals. This association, present from the earliest opium-smoking exposés, increasingly eclipsed popular associations of drugs with other social groups, particularly the upper classes.

The disappearance of narcotic-laden home remedies removed addiction farther from the experience of ordinary men and women. The Pure Food and Drug Act drastically curtailed the use and potency of these over-the-counter tonics, cures, and elixirs and ultimately destined them for extinction. In the absence of first-hand experience, addiction came to be seen as something repellant, perverse, and alien. The incipient withdrawal of public sympathy is reflected in a Denver police officer's explanation of practices employed in dealing with "dopesters": "You see, the police are always keeping an eye on them. If there is any trouble of any kind they will run in a bunch of them on general principles."[27]

The Harrison Act:
Prelude to Comprehensive State Regulation

On December 17, 1914, President Woodrow Wilson signed HR 6282, the Harrison Act. The act required records of all transactions in cocaine and opiates, although it made liberal exceptions for weaker patent medicines. The Harrison Act was the product of over four years of lobbying and negotiation to make the bill acceptable to the medical and drug associations. The act was primarily intended to demonstrate the good faith of the United States in its attempts to lead an international campaign against opium, and consequently to enhance Chinese receptivity to American commercial advances.[28] Once the objections of special interest groups were met, the anti-narcotic legislation passed. Testimony to domestic dangers was primarily meant to reinforce the need to restrict narcotics. In the shadow of the widening war in Europe and the campaign against alcohol, the hurried passage of the Harrison Act was scarcely noted by the press.

President Taft had cited the "chaotic condition" of state laws "designed to minimize the drug-habit evil" in his message transmitting to Congress his secretary of state's 1912 report on the opium traffic. The country's "enormous misuse of opium and the habit-forming drugs," the president warned, was attributable in part to "ineffective state laws, as well as the inability of states with good laws to protect themselves against the clandestine introduction of the drugs from neighboring or distant States, and therefore in a larger sense to the lack of control of the Federal Government of the importation, manufacture, and interstate traffic in them." To progressive legislators who had extended federal control under the interstate commerce clause to cover white slavery, prize fights, films, and the products of child labor, controlling interstate traffic in narcotics seemed natural. Neither did they doubt that the constitutional reservation to the states of powers not granted the federal government precluded federal authorities from dealing with matters wholly within the boundaries of a single state.[29]

The Harrison Act was expected to bolster the defenses of states with potentially effective anti-narcotic laws but swamped by the flow of narcotics from neighboring states with laxer laws or enforcement. Harrison Act sponsors and professional associations, whose approval insured passage, clearly believed that, beyond this limited measure of federal assistance, responsibility for the "distribution of these habit-forming drugs to the actual consumers" belonged "exclusively to the province of the states themselves." Dr. James R. Beal, both a lawyer and a physician and the primary representative of the APhA in the negotiation of an anti-narcotic bill, made this point unmistakably:

> All that the Federal authority can do is to provide the means whereby, through registration, etc., the quantity and character of the drugs can be traced to the last distributor and to make this information available to state, territorial and municipal officers. If the States fail to adopt proper statute regulations, or if their officials fail to properly enforce the local laws, then the Federal enactment will have but little effect in controlling improper use of the named narcotic drugs.

Beal added that, even as written, some of the record-keeping requirements and limits on prescriptions might infringe the states' exclusive police powers.[30]

Given this widespread acknowledgment of the limits of federal activity, efforts to provide Colorado with a comprehensive anti-narcotic statute naturally proceeded apace with negotiations for an acceptable federal act. The Colorado law, passed four months after the Harrison Act in April of 1915, was closely fitted to the provisions of the federal law. The national convention of the APhA had met in Denver in October of 1912 and called for a convocation of the drug trades to influence the expected federal legislation. The convention stirred the interest of the APhA's local affiliate, the Colorado Pharmacal Association (CPA), and the Colorado medical community. In the fall of 1914, the annual meeting of the Colorado State Medical Society received the reports of its Committee to Cooperate with the State Pharmacal Association. The committee reported the "urgent need for legislation for curtailing the sale and use of habit-forming drugs, and providing for the care of those already addicted to their use by the establishment of suitable quarters for their proper treatment and care at public expense." The committee also called for "voluntary or judicial commitment of such persons." It proposed that the CPA prepare and offer a bill regulating sales of habit-forming drugs and that the Medical Society draft a bill providing for treatment at public expense. "Until both measures are met," the committee concluded, "neither will be effective. To cut off the supply of these drugs to those dependent, we feel, imposes provision for treatment at option."[31]

Colorado Enacts Comprehensive Drug Control

Some six weeks after the Harrison Act's passage, a bill was introduced for a comprehensive narcotics control act, the Harrison Act serving "in the main . . . as the substance of our state law; supplement essentially relating to commitment of narcotic drug addicts and their care." The act applied, as did the Harrison Act, to transactions involving opium or coca. Certain "weak" preparations and remedies were entirely exempt if sold in good faith as medicines; other retail sales required a prescription. The rules and regulations adopted by the commissioner of Internal Revenue for implementing the Harrison Act were declared adopted for the enforcement of the Colorado act. The State Board of Health subsequently declared that all past and future rulings of the commissioner of Internal Revenue concerning the Harrison Act would be considered to have been adopted as the board's own. It is difficult to imagine a more complete melding of state and federal efforts.[32]

The state act, however, said nothing about the treatment of addicts at public expense, providing only that a record be kept by a physician who, "in the course of his professional practice and not for the purpose of evading the act," prescribed or provided a controlled drug to a habitual user. An innovative bill to provide for the cure of addicts at a state institution failed of enactment, though it reportedly had Governor Carlson's favor. The proposal, drafted by a deputy Denver city attorney, would have created a state "farm" for drug users, combining a hospital and industrial school. The patient's work was expected to be therapeutic, to support the farm, and to provide a relief fund from which the inmate's family could receive $.50 a day.[33]

The new act enabled state boards to revoke or restore the licenses of convicted professionals. First convictions were misdemeanors. Second and subsequent convictions were felonies, punishable by a term one to three years of hard labor in the state penitentiary. Corporations were subject to a fine of $1,000 to $5,000. Upon conviction, permits or licenses were forfeited, not to be renewed for five years. Together, these provisions radically stiffened control of drugs.[34]

Results of Comprehensive Control

Colorado voters had adopted statewide prohibition the previous fall, to be effective January 1, 1916, so the unopposed passage of the narcotics act was unremarkable. It had been anticipated that the Harrison Act's enforcement would result in "a besieging of hospitals by drug addicts and a crime wave of national scope accompanied by a trail of suicide and death." These dire consequences did not materialize, in part because, as several knowledgeable observers suggested, the extent of addiction was considerably exaggerated. "In recent years," observed Martin I. Wilbert of the Agriculture Department's Bureau of Chemistry, "social workers, reformers, and newspaper writers generally have seemed to vie with each other in the presentation of startling data regarding the number and kind of drug addicts in the country." The number of addicts who could be maintained for the amount of opium and coca legitimately imported—and prior to the Harrison Act there was little reason for smuggling—simply did not approximate the one to two percent of the population estimated to be addicted.[35]

Three other factors minimized any immediate outcry from addicts whose usual source of supply was dried up by the Harrison Act. A provision in both the Colorado and federal acts allowed administration of narcotics to addicts "in the course of professional treatment." This was understood by many reputable physicians as in no way restricting maintenance of addicts under their care. Addicts able to afford professional care might thereby avoid or at least postpone withdrawal. In addition, many cities responded by organizing clinics and special hospitals. Denver had assisted in preparing the proposal for treatment at state expense, which was subsequently lost in the legislature. In the summer of 1915 Denver's civic and religious leaders launched a campaign to raise $25,000 to create a "Rest Haven" for the "regeneration of City Drug Fiends." Hospitals and jails were crowded and of little help, and although ample treatment was available for those who could pay, "the user of drugs alone [of all unfortunates] has no place to turn for succor." The organizers appealed to the civic pride of Denver's citizens, pointing out that many eastern cities and states had already acted, and that the campaign had "the heart interest of the upbuilders and uplifters of Denver." This effort by responsible citizens came to nothing, but others had acted even more promptly to meet the needs of the city's addicts.[36]

In late April, Internal Revenue agents assisted by city health inspectors arrested a Denver plumber and his son as the organizers of what newspapers called "the dope trust," supplying heroin and cocaine to retail peddlers. The case received considerable attention as the city's first experience with large-scale traffic in the wake of the Harrison Act. Heroin tablets smuggled into the United States and bought in Philadelphia at $1.15 per thousand sold in Denver for $50; a packet of cocaine costing the trust $.06 brought $1. Persistent reports of addiction among the well-to-do appeared to be confirmed by agents' descriptions of the trust's two evening distribution routes—one downtown and one through the fashionable neighborhoods of Capitol Hill, where domestic servants were reported to "make purchases of heroin for their mistresses." The lure of huge profits assured a ready supply of successors to the trust. Subsequent accounts of raids and arrests rapidly took on a repetitious dullness, sparked only by the supposed value of the contraband drugs and the increasing ingenuity of their hiding places.[37]

Saving the Indian from Peyote

Three acts passed in the spring of 1917 to control *Cannabis indica*, chloral hydrate, and peyote evidenced the continuing strength of the reforming temper in Colorado on the eve of America's entry into the First World War. Peyote use had apparently spread northward in the last two decades of the nineteenth century from Indians living along the Rio Grande in Mexico. Peyote was first reported in 1883 as *Anhalonium Lewinii* and by the early 1890s had become a source of concern to the Bureau of Indian Affairs (BIA) because of its use among the Kiowa in Oklahoma. Colorado's prohibition of alcoholic beverages—in effect at midnight on January 1, 1916—had been received uneventfully, although with limited enthusiasm in Denver. In this climate, the campaign to rescue Colorado's Indians from the debilitating effects of peyote seemed natural. The campaign exemplifies the progressive commitment to advance the welfare of those deemed less competent and less fortunate.

In 1916 both houses of Congress had considered but failed to pass a bill to prohibit peyote use. Colorado apparently acted because of the failure of federal legislation. Mrs. S.A.R. Brown, "socially prominent" in Denver, led the efforts of concerned women in the city and throughout the state in promoting a bill endorsed by more than a dozen women's organizations and other civic groups, including the National Mother's Congress, the Parent Teacher Association, the Women's Christian Temperance Union, the Women's Club, the Association of Collegiate Alumnae, and the Ministerial Alliance of over 140 Denver churches. With this backing, the bill, introduced by Congressman Clem Crowley of Denver on January 11, passed both houses unopposed and received the governor's signature in less than seven weeks. The act began with a rather extraordinary declaration that the use of anhalonium, or peyote, in Colorado was "dangerous to the life, liberty, property, health, education, morals and safety of the citizens of this state, and is inconsistent with the good order, peace and safety of the state." Stiff penalties were provided for both individual and corporate offenders. Curiously, the use of peyote by Indians in Colorado was still unknown to the BIA two years later.[38]

Peyote rapidly returned to the role of exotic filler for Denver's Sunday newspapers, a role it had held since before the turn of the century. In 1899 the *Denver Times* had published an extensive account datelined Washington, D.C., and captioned "Would Make Hop Fiends Envious." It appeared, however, well back in the ladies' section below a larger item, "Fashions Call for Skirts in New Mode." The article oddly conveyed both the assessment of a Smithsonian ethnologist who characterized peyote use as "a saturnalian revel in an artistic wonderland" and the BIA's condemnation of it as "ruinous to both body and mind." Ultimately, the anti-peyote campaigns of 1916 and 1917 in Washington, D.C., and Colorado, Utah, and other western states generated no more than passing public concern. The campaigns seem to have been led by one of the national organizations concerned with Indian welfare, most likely the Home Mission Council of North America, to whom the quasi-Christian ritual use of peyote was especially objectionable. Despite the prominent emphasis on the "killing of dozens of Indians yearly," the *Post* in 1917 treated the peyote story as a society or women's feature. The same issue termed a contemporary Oklahoma bill to ban smoking or the sale of tobacco "drastic." Buffalo Bill's funeral, by contrast, claimed front-page treatment in the issue that carried both the peyote and tobacco stories.[39]

Saving the "Mexican" from Marijuana

With the peyote bill still in committee, on January 30, 1917, state representative Andres Lucero of Las Animas County introduced a bill to prohibit the cultivation of *Cannabis sativa*. Two days later he introduced a companion measure to outlaw traffic in *Cannabis indica* and chloral hydrate by adding them to the list of substances controlled by the comprehensive narcotic act of 1915. Social and economic developments more readily explained the concern over marijuana. By 1917 the wartime demand that eventually more than doubled Colorado's wheat and sugar beet production had already increased the demand for field labor, particularly in the labor-intensive cultivation of sugar beets. "Foreign white stock" of "Mexican origin" in Colorado increased from 3,330 in 1910 to 14,533 in 1920, 10,894 of them foreign born. These figures suggest an even greater tide of seasonal labor unrecorded by the census. Sponsorship of the bills by Lucero, who represented one of the southern tier of "Spanish" counties, reflected the sensitivity of Colorado's long-established Hispanic community to attention focused on the influx of laborers from Mexico. Colorado's Hispanic community was particularly sensitive to the use of marijuana, brought by these field workers. They were likely aware of the adverse view of marijuana long held by the upper classes in Mexico, where legislation against the plant dated from the 1880s.[40]

Lucero's bill, "to declare unlawful the planting, cultivating, harvesting, drying, curing or preparation for sale or gift of cannabis sativa," suggests origins closer to home. Cultivation was clearly a local concern. Further, the bill was directed against "cannabis sativa also known as cannabis indica, Indian hemp and *marijuana*" (emphasis added) and provided only mild penalties for "any person who shall grow or use cannabis sativa . . . that he has grown." This provision, in conjunction with the ban on sales, should have precluded all use of the plant.

These two anti-cannabis laws were not necessarily the product of circumstances peculiar to Colorado or the Southwest. Between 1913 and

1915 legislation restricting cannabis passed in eight states prior to Colorado's acts. All four of these states east of the Mississippi, including three in New England, had, in fact, acted slightly in advance of the western states. Control of cannabis had been considered in preparing the Harrison Act, and the commissioner of Internal Revenue had called for its inclusion, along with chloral hydrate, less than four months after the act took effect.[41]

Cannabis, generally in the form of hashish, the concentrated resin, had become known in Europe early in the nineteenth century as an exotic vice encountered in the course of colonial ventures in India, North Africa, and the Middle East. By mid-century, at a time when opiates provided the only effective general sedatives and analgesics, preparations of cannabis had achieved popularity as therapeutic agents. Cannabis, generally in an alcoholic tincture, had been looked to as a nonaddictive substitute for opiates. But professional interest faded rapidly when synthetic hypnotics and analgesics were developed, beginning with the widespread use of chloral hydrate in 1869. Cannabis had proved less effective than the opiates as an analgesic and unpredictable in its psychoactive effects, which predominated at therapeutic doses.[42] Nevertheless, a considerable body of professional literature dealing with cannabis existed by the turn of the century, particularly in Europe. Cannabis was known as one of the narcotics, in the broad sense of the term used at that time. Tincture of cannabis was available at most pharmacies and was occasionally recommended by physicians as a mild sedative. It was against cannabis in medicinal preparations that the earlier eastern state laws seem to have been directed.

If white Americans in the nineteenth century knew anything of cannabis as an exhilarant or euphoriant, they knew it through such literary works as Dumas' *Count of Monte Cristo* and the "confessions" of Fitz Hugh Ludlow, an early American sampler of psychoactive substances. The practice of smoking the dried leaves and flowering tops seems not to have been widely recognized in the United States until the early 1920s. Black slaves, however, almost certainly brought the practice from Africa to the South, where hemp—cannabis—had been a common field crop since the seventeenth century. The first reliable report of smoking marijuana was of use among enlisted men serving in the Canal Zone in 1916, although troops under General Pershing's command during the punitive raid into Mexico in 1914 probably encountered the practice.[43] Certainly Pancho Villa's men relished the affront to their social betters in "La Cucaracha," a song that immortalized them as cockroaches who could not march without their marijuana. By the early 1920s marijuana use was common among dock laborers and sailors in eastern and Gulf Coast ports.

Congressman Lucero may have received assistance in drafting his bill banning traffic in cannabis and chloral by amending the comprehensive act of 1915. At least as early as 1914, Harry V. Williamson, chief of the Denver district office of the Treasury Department's Narcotics Division, had pressed for laws against cannabis. In light of the appeal for marijuana control earlier that year by the commissioner of Internal Revenue, his involvement seems entirely likely. The federal Bureau of Chemistry had concluded in the spring of 1918 that control of hemp under the Pure Food and Drug Act was impossible. The bureau consequently forwarded its hemp files to the Bureau of Internal Revenue for use in preparing an amendment to the Harrison Act.[44] When the Colorado legislature met again in the spring of 1919, it repealed Lucero's amendment, which had added cannabis and chloral to the list of substances controlled by the state's "Little Harrison Act" of 1915. Nothing indicated that federal failure to amend the Harrison Act to include cannabis and chloral had undermined enforcement of such provisions in Colorado's own act, whose enforcement was explicitly linked to the federal act. Without federal action, Colorado shrank from proceeding independently.[45]

The courts had extended the application of the Harrison Act in several fundamental ways, but they firmly rejected the argument that treaty obligations justified regulating local medical practices. As a result, the government could only justify the act and its regulatory effect as a revenue measure, its nominal purpose. But cannabis was homegrown and used medically with decreasing frequency. There was little indication that it moved in interstate commerce in significant quantities. A way to control cannabis without undermining the constitutionality of the entire federal drug control effort would not, in fact, be devised for another twenty years.

Failure to establish federal regulation of cannabis explains the repeal of Colorado's first control measure. The failure to replace the re-

pealed statute with an independent statute is harder to explain. Colorado was left in the peculiar position of forbidding the growing of marijuana and its use by the grower, but allowing its sale and use by others.
Public concern with narcotics did rise slowly but steadily throughout
the nation during the years following the passage of the Harrison Act,
fed by newspaper accounts of raids and by statistics released by Narcotics Division agents. But the discovery that the drug habit was apparently much less common in Colorado than supposed calmed public fears.
More importantly, the contemporary effort to secure national prohibition of alcohol further diverted attention from drugs.

The first two decades of the twentieth century saw the peak of municipal efforts to regulate illicit drugs as poisons and as a vice and to
provide for the cure and rehabilitation of addicts. Reformers, knowing
only too well the limitations of municipal efforts, looked with hope for
state action in both control and cure. Many believed that the Harrison
Act had provided the solid foundation upon which state regulation could
be effective. Colorado took its lead for legislation and enforcement from
the Harrison Act, as it had earlier from the federal Pure Food and Drug
Act. This reliance on federal initiative would rapidly evolve into depen-
dence—and ultimately into a near complete abdication of responsibility.

On February 6, 1927, The Denver Post *ran this photograph with the caption, "DESTROYING COSTLY DOPE: Internal Revenue Department Agents, in Washington, D.C., Disposing, Finally, of a Large Quantity of Drugs Seized in the Raids."* Colorado Historical Society.

Chapter Three

The Expanding Federal Role

FTER THE Great War, Colorado struggled with a slackening economy that exacerbated racial, social, and labor tensions. But the early years of the post-war decade were marked by relative public indifference to illicit drug use. Indeed, in the first years of prohibition, federal drug authorities encountered active resistance to efforts to extend their control. The privileged doctor-patient relationship and state regulation of the medical practice barred the way. In this climate a series of little-noticed court cases quietly consolidated and extended the federal role initiated by the Harrison Act. By the mid-1920s, the growing difficulty of enforcing prohibition preoccupied the federal government. But in Colorado, the drug habits of Indians and Hispanics caused growing concern. Colorado played a significant role in the extension of federal control over marijuana in the 1930s.

Implementing the Harrison Act

In early 1915, when the district collector of internal revenue notified Colorado physicians of the regulations the Harrison Act imposed, optimism outweighed irritation with the new record-keeping requirements. The Colorado State Medical Society reprinted a Public Health officer's optimistic assessment that "now that dope is not easily gotten by 'fiends,'" cures were much more likely and "up to the physician in individual cases." Interested physicians were referred to a bibliography on treatment in the current issue of the *Journal of the American Medical Association*.[1] Initial court decisions did, indeed, reject the federal claim that broad police powers were justified because the act fulfilled a treaty obligation. In *U.S. v. Jin Fuey Moy*, 1916, the Court found that the Harrison Act had not been passed in fulfillment of a treaty obligation, and that the attempt to criminalize possession and prescription for maintenance would be unjustifiable even if it had.

A Growing National Menace, but Reassurance for Colorado

In the spring of 1919, the Treasury Department released the report of its Special Committee to Investigate Traffic in Narcotic Drugs. Although the department could not "vouch for the accuracy of the figures given nor assume finality for the conclusions arrived at" because "complete and accurate statistics of the extent of drug addiction have never been compiled," the report was encouraging to Colorado law enforcement officers and physicians. The *Times* captioned its account: "US Finds Drug Addiction Less Thru Colorado—Denver's Record is Enviable Among Larger Cities—Dry Laws Decrease Habit, Report Declares." The committee's report, the most methodical to that time, estimated more than a million addicts throughout the United States. Although drug use was increasing nationally—fed by a widespread smuggling organization—Denver was one of the few cities where drug traffic was not increasing. Usage was in fact decreasing throughout Colorado, Wyoming, New Mexico, and Arizona, the states of the Thirteenth Internal Revenue District. The western states that had gone dry in advance of national prohibition were cited as proof that prohibition of alcohol would not increase drug use.[2]

The Treasury report also challenged conventional wisdom about the nature and extent of addiction, both nationally and in Colorado. The committee found no apparent relationship between nationality and addiction. With the exception of the Chinese, it was "a rare occurrence to find an addict among the immigrants on their arrival in this country." Neither was there a connection between occupation and addiction, nor, "contrary to general opinion," was addiction more common among females than males, but rather equally prevalent. Replies from 30.6 percent of the physicians registered under the Harrison Act reported 73,150 addicts under treatment—a figure that suggested a national total of 237,655 addicts under treatment.[3] It is unclear how the *Times* and Internal Revenue agent A. G. Dingley arrived at their figure of 441 habitual users for Colorado and Wyoming, two-thirds of them in Colorado, 138 of them women. Nevertheless, the committee's report as interpreted by Agent Dingley clearly reassured those concerned with addiction in Colorado.

The Harrison Act Is Extended to Preempt Colorado Laws

Nationally, the Special Committee's report that addiction was on the rise worked to consolidate public support for the Bureau of Internal Revenue's efforts to prohibit the use of nonmedical narcotics. Professional associations had expected the Harrison Act to do no more than make all drug transactions a matter of record and restrict sales to legal channels. Doing so, explained a Public Health Service official, "will serve to furnish the necessary information to make State and other local laws operative . . . ." The Harrison Act, he concluded, "is not in any way designed to be a regulatory measure . . . ." Police powers to protect safety and morals were still widely understood to be reserved by the Constitution to the states. Nothing in the act criminalized either possession of narcotics without a prescription or prescribing to maintain an addict. State laws were expected to be adequate once the federal government had controlled imports and interstate traffic.[4]

The Bureau of Internal Revenue and its new Narcotics Division understood their objective differently. The regulations issued in mid-January of 1915 to implement the Harrison Act specified that some users were not eligible to register. Possession by these users without a prescription violated the law. Reformers had understood that the act would not preclude simple maintenance—meeting the needs of an addict. The regulations, however, merely voided prescriptions for quantities greater than were usually employed "in normal practice." Suppliers of drugs to addicts were arrested from the outset, despite their compliance with the act's record and tax requirements. The Bureau clearly believed that the act was intended to prohibit use by addicts. Its commissioner reported with satisfaction in 1915 that the Harrison Act's tax on smoking opium and hundred-thousand-dollar bonds for manufacturers had "prevented anyone from legally engaging in such business."[5]

The Supreme Court's unfavorable ruling in *U.S. v. Jin Fuey Moy* took the Narcotics Division by surprise. The Division responded with a campaign to raise a public outcry against both dope fiends and dope doctors, then orchestrated a series of carefully selected and managed cases to win back what had been lost.[6] In its subsequent 1919–21 decisions, the Court did in fact confirm the Division's control over the manner of dispensing narcotics, rejected maintenance without intent to cure, and ultimately rejected maintenance even *with* intent to cure. The Court's reversal reflected the decreased tolerance for nonconformity characteristic of the postwar Red Scare years.

In the calmer times of Harding's "return to normalcy," the Supreme Court substantially undercut its 1919–21 decisions. The Court responded favorably to a petition arguing that health and morals in narcotics were matters for state regulation, ruling in 1925 that the Harrison Act "says nothing of 'Addicts' and does not undertake to prescribe methods for their treatment. They are diseased and proper subjects for such treatment . . . ." But the decision came too late to offset the Division's momentum in its campaign to intimidate physicians who maintained addicts.[7]

The Harrison Act Regulates Medical Practice

By the early 1920s the Harrison Act controlled medical practice to an extent unimagined by the medical profession in 1915. Agent Dingley, explaining the new "Workings and Improvements of the Harrison Anti-Narcotic Law," was careful to stress the intent "not to interfere with or harass the reputable physician." Prescriptions for simple maintenance, however, were null. In cases of advanced age or incurable disease, "maintenance should be by public health officials only." Anticipating the effect on addicts of enforcing the broadened Harrison Act, the Treasury Department, to its credit, had supported legislation to create Public Health Service clinics first to ease addicts' distress and then to cure them.[8]

When Congress balked at providing treatment, Agent Dingley was obliged to say that long-term maintenance was "primarily a problem to be handled by the municipal and state authorities." Colorado physicians had already accepted the wisdom of institutional confinement in treating addiction. By leaving maintenance to public officials, they could escape both deception by addicts and entrapment by agents. The county health officer in Grand Junction explained his quandary: "often times" local doctors referred addicts to him, believing that he could prescribe. But the nearest hospital was 400 miles away, and he doubted his authority to prescribe for ambulatory treatment.[9]

The Extent of Addiction and Treatment

What indeed could be done to treat addiction? Denver's attempt to provide treatment through the county jail had come to little, a private effort to create a "rest haven" for addicts had failed, and the state legislature had declined to create a treatment "farm." Addicts were in fact accommodated in a wide variety of state and local institutions, but the 1921–22 report of the State Detention Home for Women with Venereal Disease indicates the makeshift nature of these arrangements. The home reported thirty-seven drug addicts admitted. "We have exceeded our authority in taking some of these cases . . . at the earnest solicitation of the Federal Narcotic officers," wrote the superintendent. But "these cases were hopeful ones and having no money, we were urged to give them a chance. Six of these cases were permanently cured." The next biennial report noted eight more cures confirmed by federal agents. The women's desperation for a "chance" may be gauged by the reported condition of the home—rotting wood and disintegrating plaster. From its earliest years, the State Insane Asylum at Pueblo had reported a few drug-related admissions every year—either simple addiction or drug-induced insanity. An early peak of six drug-related cases in a total of 243 admissions for 1891–92 was not exceeded until an exceptional spurt to eight cases for 1921–22.[10]

The modernization that changed the Board of Lunacy Commissioners to the State Board of Corrections and the Insane Asylum to the State Hospital did not, however, change admission practices. The hospital's new superintendent complained that the new law "[threw] off all restrictions as to who may be committed," allowing local judges and officials to require the hospital to accept many who were quite sane but needed custodial care. Neither did creation in 1921 of a Food and Drug Division in the State Board of Health improve the care of addicts. Neglect of addicts was hardly surprising: the state provided poorly for the mentally ill, who were more likely to enjoy public sympathy. Superintendent LaMoure complained persistently and with growing bitterness about the wretched inadequacy of the state's care. By his estimate, Colorado made the lowest per capita expenditure in the nation. Indeed, Colorado trailed the nation in expenditure for all public health services, being one of only two states in 1924 without a division of child hygiene. The state's feeble public health effort, a sad counterpoint to the glittering fortunes amassed from its mineral wealth, was bolstered only when New Deal and wartime programs infused federal funds.[11]

With no special provision for their treatment, addicts were accommodated in state hospitals, the reformatory at Buena Vista, the penitentiary at Canon City, and in county and municipal hospitals. Legislators may have hesitated to pay for a specialized hospital for addicts because they believed the Colorado Psychopathic Hospital in Denver, opened in 1925, would meet the need. Theories of abnormal psychology enjoyed a wide acceptance among both professionals and the public as the key to understanding and managing a range of deviant behavior. The increasingly popular view of addicts as weaklings, degenerates, or criminals also surfaced in professional writing, often under a mantle of Freudian nomenclature. Dr. Lawrence Kolb, one of the most capable students of addiction in the 1920s, found that "carefree individuals, devoted to pleasure, seeking new sensation," constituted nearly half of the 86 percent of those addicted for "abnormal" reasons. But Dr. George S. Johnson reported to the Colorado Medical Society in 1927 that treatment of drug addiction remained a psychiatric problem and was becoming "increasingly difficult," as the laws kept the stable but not the unstable away from drugs and had already forced the cure of the most tractable cases.[12]

Fear of Addicts Withers Public Sympathy for Peyote Users

Protection from addicts, rather than treatment for addiction, increasingly preoccupied the public in the 1920s. The change in public sentiment was most apparent in the regulation of peyote. Legislation to restrict peyote and marijuana use had been enacted in 1917 with relatively little evidence of public concern—in the case of peyote, irresponsible Indians were to be rescued from the effects of a debilitating vice. Five years later, it was belatedly discovered that Colorado's law would not control sale of peyote on reservations. Colorado's Indians had neither increased nor left their remote rural homes in significant numbers, but great urgency pervaded the call for legislative action. Speaking to the House Judiciary Committee in 1922, Congressman Edward T. Taylor buttressed his plea for federal action with a fearsome description of the drug's effects. Taylor told the committee that "a few drops of the concoction would 'make a rabbit spit in a bulldog's face'" and that "its effects on Indians is to enthuse them with a desire to whip the universe."[13] Usage may or may not have grown with the increased difficulty of obtaining bootleg whiskey, as Congressman Taylor also suggested. The altered perception of peyote's effects reflected changes among whites, not Indians.

Reining in "Marijuana-Crazed Mexicans"

Public attention in Colorado soon turned not to what Indians on peyote might do on the reservation, but to what Hispanics using "marihuana" might do in the state's cities and migrant camps. Colorado's experience with marijuana displays the recurring association of a psychoactive drug with a particular ethnic minority, stigmatizing both the drug as "dope" and the group as users. Colorado prominently influenced national attitudes towards marijuana and significantly shaped the legislative and judicial response.

Abuse of medicinal preparations had motivated Colorado's first effort to control cannabis in 1917. But by the early 1920s, cannabis had come to be known and smoked as marijuana. The press and public officials portrayed it as the supreme inciter of violence and madness. Significantly, it was federal narcotic agent Harry V. Williamson who suggested that a "Mexican shootout" in Denver might have been caused by marijuana. Against marijuana, he regretted to say, federal officers were powerless to act. With marijuana as with intoxicating liquors, Williamson said, the user passed through various stages, from "slight exhilaration to downright ugliness," but there the comparison stopped. Marijuana made its users "quarrelsome and often desperate," so that when "Mexicans fight each other they are apt to be full of marihuana." "It is far more deadly in its effects than either cocaine or morphine," he warned, "especially as far as danger to innocent parties is concerned." Indeed, dope fiends rejected it because it "made them feel too ugly and desperate." City officials were at a loss to know how to deal with the drug, because "no law against its use nor against its sale" existed. But Denver police were preparing to mop up marijuana by "a general cleanup of the Mexican quarters."[14]

The casual readiness of Denver police to proceed without statutory basis was characteristic of the times. Post-war tensions and economic malaise also fed the Ku Klux Klan's brief but surprising flowering in Colorado. Nearly twenty years earlier a physician in the San Luis Valley, then the center of Colorado's "Spanish" population, had offered a sad but eloquent assessment:

> The Mexicans know, and we know, that even-handed justice is not dealt out to them. White men may stagger down the streets drunk, or engage in brawls and fist fights at noonday, unmolested and unpunished, but the Mexican is promptly "run in." They are imposed upon, defrauded, assaulted and even murdered and look in vain for justice.

Denver's "foreign white stock of Mexican origin" had increased from 273 in 1910 to 1,783 in 1920, still only a small fraction of a total population of 104,850. Given the tendency to under-count minorities and migrants, however, this more than sixfold increase suggests an even larger addition to the city's Hispanic population. The rapidity of the increase and the labor glut of the post-war slump, compounded by men returning from service, intensified resentment against Hispanics.[15]

Marijuana and Mexicans were among the concerns of a federal grand jury report of 1922, which found the drug traffic in Denver "appalling" and recommended deportation of "all aliens who peddle narcotics." The *Denver Times*, touching the most sensitive aspects of public concern, captioned its front-page account of the report, "Drugs Sold to Denver High School Pupils . . . ." Still, the depth of public concern is difficult to gauge. After the successful enactment of state and national prohibition of alcohol, the Women's Christian Temperance Union might have been expected to throw its weight against drugs. But the WCTU's *Colorado Messenger* spared only passing references to narcotics, in which they included nicotine. Nor does the Denver Women's Club, active in social uplift, seem to have directed any of its activities against drugs.[16]

Concern with marijuana was sufficient to motivate a city ordinance of 1922 prohibiting the sale, possession or use of cocaine, "cocoa [*sic*] leaves," opiates, "cannabis Indica or 'Marihuana' or any habit-forming drug or habit-forming herb." Apart from adding cannabis and "habit-forming herbs" to the list of controlled substances and raising the penalties moderately, the ordinance is of interest for authorizing impoundment of any vehicle used in illegal drug traffic.[17] Criminals had begun to use automobiles before even federal narcotic agents had been issued them or could afford them. This narcotic ordinance was Denver's last for over twenty-five years, so swiftly was narcotics control moving upward.

Federal Agents Successfully Ride the Statistics

Within a few years of the Harrison Act's passage, press attention to narcotics focused on activities of federal agents. Although the Narcotics Division field force was small, its Denver office staff (responsible for Wyoming, Utah, and New Mexico as well as Colorado) easily overshadowed local enforcement. The state had no officers committed exclusively to narcotics, and Denver had allocated only a fraction of two detectives' time. This disparity was even more pronounced when the Volstead Act of December 22, 1919, incorporated the Narcotics Division into the Treasury's newly created Prohibition Unit, doubling the Division's budget. By 1928 the Denver office of the Narcotics Division employed a staff of thirteen, compared to fifty-one employees enforcing the prohibition of alcohol.[18]

In addition to a larger staff and the glamour of battling the big dealers, the Division office enjoyed a near monopoly of the statistics by which the shadowy evils of addiction and trafficking were fleshed out for the public. Even ignoring the vagaries of definition and compilation, the significance of arrest, conviction, and seizure statistics was unclear. A fifty percent increase in reported violations could be read, as the commissioner of Internal Revenue did in 1922, as "indicating a more effective operation of the field force." Or, it could be read as a monstrous increase in drug abuse, demanding increased appropriations. An increase in quantities of drugs seized could be portrayed as evidence that the traffic was being stamped out, or that it was mushrooming out of control. One should read in this light the good news from Acting Agent-in-Charge H. B. Westover, passed on by the *Denver Post*: " 'Dope' Traffic Sharply Suppressed in Colorado—Consumption of Habit-Forming Drugs Less by 65 Per Cent in the Last Twelve Months Owing to Activities of Federal Agents and Court."[19]

Calculating such a figure is virtually inconceivable, but Agent Westover's confidence seems to have rested on the near quadrupling of "wholesale" dope prices in two years: "The high price of the stuff, which soared on account of what might be called the high mortality among peddlers, is prohibitive to all but a few addicts," he concluded. "As a result many are taking cures and many have left Colorado." Westover had disproved "utterly false reports that the dope evil had made its appearance in our high schools." Nor had Denver and Colorado Springs society been giving fashionable "snow" (cocaine) parties. "In all," Westover concluded, "Colorado is so free from dope that it can be said that there is no state with better conditions prevailing than here." In this achievement the Division's five agents had been "helped," he said, by the "cooperation of the police throughout the state" and the tough sentences of federal judge J. Foster Symes. Two years later, Agent Westover read in the near doubling of the previous year's number of arrests, convictions, and sentences evidence of the most effective "drive" to date and confirmation that the "dope fiend has almost entirely disappeared from Denver."[20]

The pitfalls in extrapolating from enforcement figures to the actual use of illicit drugs are evident in the figures for 1925, Agent Westover's banner year for enforcement activities. Reported violations by unregistered persons jumped from 47 the previous year to 119; convictions of unregistered violators from 49 to 97; aggregate sentences from 27 to 78 years; and total fines from $2,215 to $17,875. But drugs seized dropped from 128 ounces to 61 ounces. That same year, arrests for violations of the Volstead Act doubled, and stills seized increased by a factor of five—but gallons of liquor seized increased by only about forty percent. The rough doubling in enforcement activities against both narcotics and alcohol, accompanied by disproportionately small increases in alcohol seized and an absolute decrease in narcotics seized, do not suggest an increase in illicit activity. They suggest that political pressures on the Treasury or internal bureaucratic imperatives required a demonstrable increase in enforcement—achieved by sweeping up small "kitchen sink" distillers and non-dealing addicts previously ignored.[21]

Federal statistics, however, made much poorer reading than drug-related arrests and exposés. The newspapers had discovered the appeal of drug stories and typically treated them in a manner calculated to titillate readers with tales of danger and the exotic. "US Dope Ring Traced to Colorado" captioned a front-page account of two men seized in Denver with $1,200 worth of opium. The contraband, Agent Westover said, linked them to "the largest wholesale narcotics ring ever discovered." A closer reading revealed that the two men were linked to the ring only as customers and to Colorado by being plucked from a train en route from Oregon. In 1926 and 1927 the *Denver Post* carried a dozen installments of "My Thrills and Horrors as a Drug Slave," the confessions of a previously addicted actress. Excursions into the world of the bootlegger and the speakeasy were also typical Sunday supplement fare.[22]

From "My Thrills and Horrors as a Drug Slave," Denver Post, February 6, 1927. For several weeks, the twelve-part serial ran alongside an exposé of bootleggers' activities entitled "Sinister Secrets of America's Night Clubs." Colorado Historical Society.

Action against the Menace of Mexicans and Marijuana

The Harrison Act's success in controlling opium and cocaine may be debated. But neither federal law nor, for practical purposes, state law had even attempted to restrict marijuana. In the 1920s the swelling immigration of Mexicans to Colorado spurred proposals for control. In January of 1927, two representatives from Pueblo introduced a bill to ban growing, possessing, selling, or giving away "Cannabis Indica, or Cannabis Sativa, commonly known as Indian Hemp, Hasheesh or Marijuana." Pueblo was an understandable source for such a bill. By 1930 Pueblo County ranked third behind Weld and Denver counties in "Mexican" residents. With 3,356, the city of Pueblo was nearly twenty percent "Mexican." The Pueblo bill found cannabis to be a "habit-forming drug, the unrestricted use of which is injurious to the well-being of the users." The bill proposed to repeal the act of 1917 prohibiting cultivation, and instead to regulate sales to pharmaceutical manufacturers, wholesale druggists, retail druggists, and consumers upon prescription, and of weak preparations "suitable only for external use." Infractions were punishable by fines of $50 to $300 and imprisonment in the county jail for one to six months.[23]

First referred to the Committee on Indian and Military Affairs, presumably because Mexicans and Indians were "similar," the bill was eventually reported upon favorably by the Committee on Medical Affairs. After the bill passed unopposed, the House accepted the request of Congressman Pedro A. Gonzales of Huerfano and Costilla Counties to add his name as a sponsor. Gonzales' request reflects the determination of Colorado's longtime "Spanish" residents to disassociate themselves from the Mexican newcomers, most of them laborers, and from their repellant new vice. Still, violation of the act was only a misdemeanor. Minimum penalties of $50 and one month appear to have hedged against judges taking the offense too lightly.[24]

Even as the anti-marijuana bill was moving unopposed toward passage, Denver authorities announced a new "drive" against the sale of marijuana. The results were apparent from time to time in Denver press accounts of the arrests of small-time growers and sellers, often with Hispanic surnames. Colorado's increased concern also contributed to an emerging national interest in marijuana. Colorado was newly aware of marijuana as a vice of Mexican laborers that occasionally led to Saturday night violence. National material appearing in the Denver press, however, had a markedly different flavor. Again, the Sunday magazine section proved well-suited for sketching a new menace. The *Post* breathlessly informed its readers about "A Home Grown Drug that Drives Its Victims Mad—Raised in Any Backyard and Smoked in Cigarettes, Marihuana Is the Most Deadly Narcotic Now Fought by the U.S." Leading to "violence and later to a fiendish desire to mutilate or kill," hemp would drive all but the strongest insane in a third the time that opium would kill. In contrast, a syndicated article titillated readers with a glimpse of Greenwich Village, where, in "a certain set, no party is considered complete without the drug." "Marihuana smoking," said the author, "appeals to a certain bohemian, free-thinking, imaginative group of artists, writers, musicians and others who form an aesthetic group in New York's Latin Quarter."[25]

A Denver reporter suggested the roots of drug legislation in ethnic divisions: "When a peon has smoked a pipeful of it he turns completely insane, runs amuck—and kills." The chronic effect in whites was insanity, but in the more primitive brain of the "Mexican," the article observed, a single pipeful would work its deadly effect. The observation needed no further explanation. In the 1920s, scientific and popular belief in a racial hierarchy was almost universal and contributed to both the Immigration Restriction Act of 1922 and the revival of the Ku Klux Klan in such states as Indiana, Oregon, and Colorado. Similarly, prohibition of alcohol had earlier been supported by many who expected to continue to drink. They had meant to deny alcohol to those of unsteady habits, particularly recent immigrants concentrated in inner cities who drank the wrong beverages at the wrong times and places. This point was made by Senator Carle W. Burke of Denver, who introduced a bill to ban public intoxication with drugs or alcohol *outside* incorporated areas. He buttressed his case with the observation that, "No objection to the bill should come from the Republican majority," as previously "the Republicans have drunk all the whiskey and the Democrats have assumed all the responsibility."[26]

Colorado both contributed to and was influenced by marijuana's emerging national reputation as a drug of unparalleled menace. Nevertheless, local considerations motivated the legislature's toughening of marijuana penalties in 1929. Denver's city chaplain had warned that seasonal Mexican workers brought in 4,500 pounds in 1928 and would bring in 6,500 in 1929. Only a penitentiary sentence, he said, would deter dealers. Senator Ray Talbot, cosponsor of the 1927 marijuana bill, joined a Pueblo colleague and two Denver-area senators to introduce a bill increasing penalties. Finally, the Senate amended the 1927 act to make second and subsequent convictions felonies punishable by one to five years in the state penitentiary—serious penalties indeed. The bill passed both houses unopposed and received Governor Adams' signature on April 18, 1929.[27]

Roots of Federal Marijuana Legislation

Concern in Colorado over the use of marijuana had in fact grown sporadically for at least a decade prior to the act. As early as 1918, the chief federal narcotic agent in the Narcotics Division's Denver office had stressed the dangers of marijuana and called for federal controls. In the early 1920s Colorado senator Richard C. Callen had tried without success to obtain a state law banning marijuana. As United States marshal he continued his campaign, and the 1927 anti-marijuana act was introduced in the Colorado Senate on his recommendation. A week earlier, delivering prisoners east, Callen had stopped in Washington to urge Colorado's Senator Lawrence C. Phipps to back federal legislation. Action was urgent, Marshal Callen said, because many Colorado schoolchildren were becoming addicts, and marijuana had been found growing in the prison at Canon City and as far west as Grand Junction. City, state, and federal officials endorsed federal control, he said, and Denver Chief of Police R. F. Reed wanted marijuana added to the list of substances controlled by the Harrison Act. Phipps had promised to take the matter in hand.[28]

Senator Phipps had replaced progressive William C. Shafroth in the wartime election of 1918 as Colorado voters shifted their support to the Republican party. Politically conservative and a man of considerable wealth, Phipps had received the support of the Colorado Klan during its brief period of influence. The desirability of controlling a vice identified with lower-class members of an ethnic minority and with social nonconformists seems to have been self-evident, and Phipps became a leading advocate of federal control of marijuana. Certainly he acted on Marshal Callen's suggestion without delay. On January 25, 1929, Levi G. Nutt,

Commissioner of Narcotics, replied to the senator's suggestion that marijuana be controlled under the Harrison Act.

Nutt carefully explained that the Harrison Act's constitutionality rested on the production of revenue by taxing legitimate transactions in opiates and cocaine. Restricting abuse, though highly desirable, was an incidental side-effect. Because legitimate uses for *Cannabis indica* and peyote were, respectively, few and nonexistent, tax legislation "would be of doubtful constitutionality and could endanger the entire structure of narcotic control under the Harrison Act." Moreover, the abuse of cannabis and peyote appeared to be "confined to the southwestern and midwestern states, and possibly some of the larger cities." Nutt therefore suggested that "this evil may more properly be met by state and municipal legislation." "If abuse of Cannabis Indica and Peyote exist to any appreciable extent in Colorado," Nutt concluded, the state legislature could deal with it. Senator Phipps promised to bring Nutt's opinion before the Colorado legislature. He had earlier indicated his readiness to work with Senator Sheppard of Texas in preparing federal legislation, and he noted now the prospects of including marijuana and peyote in the Uniform Narcotic Drug Act, then in preparation by the Convention of Commissioners on Uniform State Laws. Phipps nevertheless continued to agitate the federal bureaucracy to take a more active role.[29]

The 1920s were characterized by a slow atrophy of state and local enforcement, while public interest in "the drug problem," particularly marijuana, became more constant. The drug menace was well established as a reliable feature for the press. News coverage and public interest had become important concerns for federal drug authorities, whose skill in press relations grew impressively. But in Colorado's post-war climate of economic distress, social tensions, and racial fears, marijuana generated genuine public concern.

Harry J. Anslinger, commissioner of the federal Bureau of Narcotics, 1930–62. Historical Collections and Labor Archives, Penn State.

Chapter Four

Marijuana and the Bureau of Narcotics

VER THE summer and fall of 1929, advocates of federal control of marijuana searched for ways to avoid infringing the states' police powers. The near impossibility of controlling marijuana under laws framed to control legitimate drug imports soon became apparent. In October the Treasury advised against Senator Sheppard's proposal to control cannabis under the Narcotic Drug Import and Export Act of 1922, the Jones-Miller Act. That act relied on simple possession as evidence of illegal importation. Because domestic cultivation was widespread, simple possession was no proof of illegal importation, and the Treasury feared that including marijuana would endanger the entire act.[1]

The Uniform Act and Rising Concern with Marijuana

By January of 1930, the Treasury and the Narcotics Division had formulated their responses. The proposed Uniform Narcotic Drug Act should prohibit, rather than restrict, the growth and sale of cannabis. The plant was so commonly grown that "it is easily seen that there must be a drastic and efficient system of internal control over the drug if the evils said to be associated with its abuse are to be averted." State laws, therefore, should be "supplemented and made more effective" by a federal law banning interstate transportation. Finally, import and export of cannabis should be banned by a separate act, which Senator Phipps promised to introduce.[2]

Nutt's contacts with the Public Health Service (PHS) explain his reluctant response to Phipps' proposals to crush the "weed of insanity and death." Preparations of cannabis, the PHS reported, offered "a mild counter-irritant," "used also for relief of neuralgic pain; to encourage sleep; and to soothe restlessness." Phipps' sole achievement was the inclusion of cannabis and peyote in the list of "habit forming narcotic drugs" whose victims would be treated at the federal narcotic "farms" authorized by Congress in January of 1929. His hopes that one of the farms would be built in Colorado were disappointed.[3]

Creation of the Bureau of Narcotics

Senator Phipps' pursuit of a federal solution to Colorado's supposed marijuana problems reflected a thorough reversal of the nation's attitudes toward drug control. When the Harrison Act had passed in 1914, drug use was unequivocally the responsibility of local authorities, who at first adamantly defended their prerogatives. But by the 1930s, lean budgets reduced state and local officers' enthusiasm for added responsibilities, and drug enforcement was readily conceded to federal agents. Federal agencies for their part increasingly fanned the flames of public concern, alternately trying to build support for extensions of their own authority and urging local authorities to act decisively against drugs. Colorado's response to illicit drugs from the late 1920s on was bound up in these curious attempts by federal and state authorities to deflect responsibility to the other.

The emergence of a single-purpose federal drug agency under an energetic, single-minded leader directly shaped Colorado's experience. Shortly after Levi Nutt resigned as Narcotics Division director, his reputation clouded by a scandal involving his son, the Division succumbed as well. On June 14, 1930, an act to improve enforcement of prohibition moved the Bureau of Prohibition from the Treasury to the Department of Justice, merging its Narcotics Division with the Federal Narcotics Control Board to form a new Bureau of Narcotics within the Treasury. On September 25, 1930, Harry J. Anslinger, a former official of the Bureau of Prohibition with minor diplomatic and consular experience, was appointed commissioner of the new Bureau of Narcotics. Anslinger later recalled that within a few weeks of his taking office, the Bureau was attacked on the Senate floor by Senator Cole Blease of South Carolina, outraged by the ease with which he had purchased smoking opium "only one block from where we are now deliberating." Anslinger responded with a series of raids to purge the District of Columbia of opium dens, aware that the Bureau's future depended on its ability "to win and hold the respect and support of Congress and the public."[4]

Challenges Facing the Bureau

The Eighteenth Amendment had authorized the states to enforce prohibition, an unprecedented provision for overlapping jurisdiction. When cities in their turn enacted prohibition ordinances, liquor violations became subject to simultaneous federal, state, and local enforcement. Denver's lack of enthusiasm disgusted state prohibition officers, as did ineffective federal efforts. One state agent was moved to write Governor Sweet, "I am not now, nor never have cooperated with the Federal Force in Colorado until they clean house and get on the job." The Bureau of Prohibition's legal section, in turn, found state narcotic laws badly lacking because they did not prohibit administering drugs to gratify addiction, revoke licenses of addicted professionals, or punish violations as felonies. Colorado, however, was one of twelve states found by the Bureau in 1923 to have "more or less complete" laws "which would be effective if enforced in connection with the Harrison Law."[5]

The states did enact a considerable number of anti-narcotic laws in the 1920s, but they pursued their own devices, and with little sense of urgency. Colorado was among the earliest sources of agitation for a federal marijuana law, but nevertheless proceeded from 1919 to 1927 with no significant state statute controlling cannabis. This lack of a sense of urgency was not confined to Colorado or to laymen. The chairman of the national Commission on Uniform State Laws had to plead for attention as he introduced the American Medical Association's exceptionally capable Dr. William C. Woodward to testify in favor of narcotics control:

> In view of the importance of the act, I think it would not be amiss to listen to the Doctor for a few minutes, that he may point out to us why it is important. In some of the states, we do not recognize the importance because it has not been called to our attention.[6]

Far more urgent was the federal failure to cut off imports of illicit narcotics. The Narcotics Division had admitted in 1927 that, while leakage of lawfully imported drugs into illicit channels had been "satisfactorily" restricted, illegal imports were now the source of almost all drugs used illicitly. Indeed, there was little prospect of stanching the flow. A year earlier, the Conference of State and Provincial Health Authorities had heard that "various companies of 'Big Fellows'" were bankrolling the import and distribution of huge quantities of narcotics. This traffic, the report argued, "should be handled exclusively by the Federal Authorities with an adequate force and not by the Police Department and the District Magistrate."[7]

Sharper critics argued that by prosecuting actual possession and use of narcotics, the Division had lapsed into "prosecuting the victims of the traffic and permitting those who reap the large monetary benefits to go untouched." Drug traffic and addiction continued to expand because, while "thousands of addicts and small peddlers have gone into the Federal prisons," for the most part the "high financiers of dope smuggling remain at large." Finally, the policing of narcotics at the points of sale and administration had been the source of ill feeling on the part of doctors and pharmacists, of which the Colorado Pharmacal Association's complaint was typical: Denver pharmacists, the association complained, were being milked through coercive "offers in compromise" by a new agent "out to make a record for himself" by stepping up enforcement.[8]

Commissioner Anslinger intended to assure critics that the policy and practice of the new Bureau of Narcotics would be entirely different. Above all, the Bureau would pursue a policy of "concentrating Federal enforcement efforts against the larger sources of supply of the illicit traffic and soliciting State action in dealing with the problems presented by the retail peddler and the existence of narcotic addicts . . . ." Federal and state enforcement activities would be complementary. Indeed, as the commissioner was to note repeatedly in the following year, Section 8 of the Act of 14 June, 1930, specifically required the Bureau to cooperate with the states in drafting legislation, exchanging information, instituting and prosecuting cases before both state and federal courts, and in bringing actions before state licensing boards.[9]

The Bureau Encounters Apathy toward Drugs

The Bureau's first year demonstrated that simply restricting federal efforts would not adequately divide the labors of narcotic enforcement. "In very few States," Anslinger reported with regret, "was any attempt made to accept a part of the burden of enforcement independently of Federal participation." More than fifteen years of federal anti-narcotic enforcement, Anslinger concluded, had created a thorough misunderstanding of jurisdiction over narcotic offenses:

> Many enforcement officers, both Federal and State, apparently had been led to believe that all narcotic cases were strictly of Federal concern. Accordingly, one of the greatest impediments to securing the application of State Laws to cases has been the fact that officials were inclined to the idea that such would be taking Federal cases into State courts. Federal agents in the field have found it difficult to overcome the misconception and to present the matter so as to bring about a thorough understanding of the dual nature of a narcotic violation, and to effect a realization that such is not only an offense cognizable by the Federal Government but is also one against which the States may legislate through the exercise of their police powers for the protection of the public health . . . .[10]

Previous federal activities against these small-time dealers and users had resulted in inefficient use of federal resources but large enforcement statistics. Now the Bureau of Narcotics was directing its efforts against smuggling, unlawful interstate traffic, and intrastate wholesalers. Although fewer federal cases were made, "these cases involved more important violations and approached nearer to the sources of drug suppliers, . . . a development attested by the longer sentences imposed upon conviction, and the greatly increased quantities of drugs seized." Indeed, the commissioner had reported as early as the end of 1930 that "increased enforcement efficiency" had accounted for a sevenfold increase in seizures, despite the bringing of fewer cases.[11]

Treasury statistics do indicate a substantial increase in seizures nationally, from 13,989 ounces of contraband in 1929 to 23,948 in 1930. But this was hardly a sevenfold increase, and seizures in 1931 dropped to 8,673 ounces. Seizures in Colorado actually dropped, from forty-five ounces in 1929 to twenty-six in 1930, while the number of unregistered violators rose from fifty-eight to seventy-three. In 1931 federal seizures in Colorado dropped further to thirteen ounces. This minute quantity nevertheless ranked Colorado sixteenth among twenty-eight states in which seizures were made. Arrests rose modestly, and sentences nearly doubled to an average of about 2.3 years. The small quantities seized and the decrease in the average penalty the following year suggest that small-time peddlers and users arrested in 1931 were the unfortunate victims of judicial severity prompted by the Bureau's purported drive against major dealers.[12]

Public concern with drugs in the early 1930s centered on marijuana, but neither drugs in general nor marijuana in particular claimed much public or official attention. Under the cloud of turmoil abroad and economic prostration and fear of crime at home, marijuana was at most a matter of shallow and intermittent public interest. The Colorado Women's Christian Temperance Union, for example, though overwhelmed by the collapse of prohibition, nevertheless cited "Mariguana" as the last of "The Seven Hatchets which are cutting the very heart out of our nation."[13] Such public concern as could be aroused over drugs did focus on marijuana and shaped the evolution of public attitudes and policy toward drugs in general.

The Denver division office of the Bureau of Narcotics reported in the spring of 1931 that the use of marijuana, "an excitant . . . comparable to cocaine" in its effects, had increased during the past five years, a fact "borne out by police records in various cities and towns of the Division." The agent believed that "not a week passes but that a user of marijuana is arrested and placed in the local city jail." All states in the division made cultivation, sale, and possession a crime. Because first-offense conviction was a misdemeanor, however, "the various State and local officers have been unable to cope with the situation," although most marijuana was grown locally rather than smuggled in or carried across state lines.[14] As there was no federal statute, the agent could only refer them to their own state laws.

Marijuana Sparks Public Interest

In the fall of 1931 the publication of the tenth and final volume of the report of the Wickersham Commission, *Crime and the Foreign Born*, roused national interest in marijuana. The *Christian Science Monitor* captioned its account of the report "Drug Used by Mexican Aliens." Press accounts repeated the commission's warning that the drug problem would be "enormously complicated by the presence of a homegrown plant containing a powerful narcotic." The author of one of the studies discounted "proof" that Mexicans were inordinately given to crime. He cited in rebuttal a California social worker's characterization of marijuana use by Mexicans as not extensive and "usually limited to unmarried men working under unendurable conditions who used it to relieve the dreariness of their existence." The Denver press, however, was more taken with the portrait of marijuana sketched by Paul L. Warnshuis, who headed the Denver office of the Presbyterian Board of National Missions. Warnshuis tried to deflect the charges of inherent criminality among Mexicans by attributing a portion of Mexican arrests to the use of marijuana. Other reports claimed that marijuana was deteriorative in its cumulative effects, induced sensations of power and the appearance of drunkenness or insanity, and was sometimes used by criminals to brace themselves before a crime.[15]

Commissioner Anslinger was into print within weeks in another *Monitor* article captioned "Narcotics Commissioner Urges Drastic Action against Hashish." The Wickersham Commission, he said, had missed the seriousness of the marijuana threat. Marijuana cigarettes could be purchased "at the corner drugstore," and criminals' use of the drug before "brutal forays" were "occurrences commonly known to the narcotics bureau." Underlining the gravity of the situation, he stressed that "California and Texas are practically the only states having restrictive legislation against the drug, and elsewhere the situation is shocking to say the least." The commissioner's statement is particularly difficult to reconcile with a compilation of state narcotic laws the PHS published the same year. The report counted twenty-one states, including Colorado, Utah, and New Mexico in the Denver division, that prohibited the sale of cannabis except upon prescription and one state, Wyoming, that prohibited all sales.[16]

Denver's Manager of Safety, Carl S. Milliken, cited marijuana as the cause of increased crime. Denver police believed marijuana was replacing opiates and cocaine among drug users. They estimated a total of several thousand Denver users of marijuana, which came mostly from the "farm districts of Adams, Morgan, and Larimer counties." Milliken called for tougher sentences and a drive against users and peddlers. Curiously, he warned that ultimately the "only means of combatting the menace is by a campaign of education," as "countless thousands of Denver citizens know nothing of marihuana or its effects" of murder and insanity.[17] The extent and nature of drug use in Colorado in the early 1930s can now, as then, only be inferred from first-hand accounts and public statistics. Beginning in 1931, the Bureau of Narcotics inquired annually about convictions under Colorado laws and was told that the state had no such statistics and no intention of compiling them. Colorado did not report enforcement statistics to the Bureau until 1941.

In Denver, home to more than a tenth of the state's population in 1930, drug arrests between 1930 and 1935 averaged about fifty a year, compared to nearly 3,000 for alcohol-related violations. In the same years drug-related arrests of those under twenty years of age averaged three per year; of those in their twenties, about twenty a year; and of those thirty and above, nearly twenty-seven a year. The figures do show a disproportionate number of drug-related arrests among young adults, comparable to a similar disproportion in alcohol-related arrests. They do not substantiate claims of the mass corruption of Denver's children. Indeed, after the 1931 peak of eight arrests of those under twenty, juvenile arrests for the remainder of the 1930s totaled only eleven.[18]

Denver's arrest and jail records do show that "Mexicans" were disproportionately represented among those arrested for drug use. "Foreign born white," a category later replaced by "Mexican" in the annual reports, accounted for almost two-thirds of Denver drug arrests between 1933 and 1935. An unusual document confirms the heavy disproportion in the number of "Mexicans" arrested for violating the city's drug laws— and the determination to define marijuana as a Mexican problem. Early in 1933 the head of the Denver office of the Bureau of Narcotics responded to Commissioner Anslinger's continuing interest in marijuana by forwarding a list of drug law violators confined in the county jail for the past nineteen months. The list was annotated with the total number of violators, eighty-seven; "Spanish and Mexican names," seventy-five; and "names of doubtful nationality (some may be Mexicans)," twelve. The agent's eagerness to demonstrate the predominance of Mexicans led him to a high count and to pen in variant spellings of "doubtful" names: "Bruce, Lee—? Brusse or Brussi;" "Monroe, Robert—? Munri?;" "Tierney, Frank—? Tierni." By any count, however, Hispanic surnames would have accounted for more than eighty percent of the total.[19]

The records of the Colorado Insane Asylum at Pueblo and the Colorado Psychopathic Hospital in Denver might be expected to substantiate the repeated warnings that drug use led to insanity. Between 1929 and 1936, the asylum admitted fifty patients with alcoholic psychoses and eight for simple addiction. Colorado Psychopathic Hospital records to 1930 reveal a total of three hundred forty cases of "exogenous toxic psychoses" attributable to the following drugs: alcohol, one hundred ninety-eight, of which nineteen died; opiates, seventy-four, of which one died; barbiturates, twenty-seven, of which two died; bromides, thirty-four, of which one died. Digitalis, ergot, "mapeline," and marijuana accounted for one case each. The hospital director stressed, not the dangers of illicit drugs, but the alarming incidence of addiction and fatality related to licit, "safe" sedatives—barbiturates and bromides, both readily available in patent medicines.[20] The absence of concern or outcry over these two drugs suggests the shallowness of popular knowledge.

The surface, at least, of Denver's public opinion was stirred from time to time by press releases from the Bureau's Denver office. In December of 1934, Joseph A. Manning, head of the Denver district office, announced a "drive" in cooperation with local police, promising that the raids would go on until all addicts and pushers were behind bars. The Denver office was clearly scraping to do its part. Nine "known addicts or pushers suspected of renewing their activities" were jailed—but no narcotics were seized, a clear indication that the drive netted only "small fry." The meager results cast light on the "800 arrests throughout the country" that Commissioner Anslinger reported to a Canadian colleague later that month.[21]

Marijuana remained the subject of desultory press attention in the early 1930s. Small items tucked well back in the papers reported the news when local police broke up a "ring," or when the efforts of the energetic executive secretary of the State Board of Health, Dr. Roy L. Cleere, led to the discovery of another marijuana "patch" or "farm." Seizures and arrests were most often reported in the counties abutting the Front Range, which contained Colorado's major cities and adjoined the state's prime agricultural land on the east.[22] The Denver district office kept the central Bureau of Narcotics supplied with clippings, statistics, and descriptions of marijuana use, often requested from Washington.

The Bureau Is Unable to Respond to Marijuana

The Bureau of Narcotics remained steadfast in its conclusion that marijuana could not be controlled under the Harrison Act. "While the Department is in entire accord with efforts to eradicate the evils associated with the abuse of cannabis," affirmed an assistant secretary of the Treasury in 1934, "it is the unanimous opinion of those engaged in the enforcement of the narcotic laws that the Congress is restricted under the Constitution from enacting legislation covering the matter which lies solely within the police power of the states."[23] As Commissioner Anslinger explained in 1934, replying to a request from a New Mexico senator for a federal marijuana law, "technical reasons" stressed by the Court in the Jin Fuey Moy decision made it "useless" to try to control possession of any domestically produced drug under the Harrison Act. Anslinger urged that "control of the traffic in marijuana may best be approached by the enactment of adequate state legislation restricting the cultivation and growth, and the sale, distribution and possession of cannabis" and by adequate enforcement.[24]

The Bureau was discovering, however, that the absence of state laws against marijuana was not the problem. When Agent Manning described the growing menace of marijuana in his district, including numerous reports of the "sale of marihuana cigarettes to young people," the Bureau asked what steps Colorado had taken to fight the new drug. Manning replied that all states in his district had laws controlling marijuana, all larger cities had ordinances under which marijuana users and traffickers could be prosecuted, and other cities proceeded under their vagrancy ordinances. "It is not the lack of law on the subject," he said, "but rather the lack of enforcement." There were many laws but "no agencies in any of the states charged directly with the enforcement of laws prohibiting the use of marihuana." Worse still, local "law enforcement officers are, more or less, political appointees and, as a consequence, change frequently, and they do not become proficient in the enforcement of any law." Even in Denver, enforcement of city and state narcotic laws and assistance in enforcement of the federal laws were part-time responsibilities.[25]

Assistant Secretary of the Treasury Gibbons shared Manning's belief that marijuana legislation was "not vigorously enforced in many of the states" because of a lack of "suitable enforcement machinery." By the fall of 1934, his estimate of the number of states with marijuana laws had risen to thirty-three, many attributable to Bureau agents' advocacy. The agents had also promoted a city ordinance for states with inadequate legislation or lax enforcement.[26] Gibbons was optimistic that the "nationwide publicity now being given to the menace" would bring appropriate legislation in the remaining states when the legislatures met the following year. His stress on the publicity campaign was consistent with his belief that "the general public has practically no knowledge of the subject of marijuana." "Local enforcement agencies in the large cities, as well as in rural communities," he regretted to say, were "in the majority of cases just as ignorant as the general public."[27] Emphasis on popular ignorance and lack of enforcement is difficult to reconcile with the Bureau's claim that the public demanded federal marijuana legislation.

The Bureau Kills Two Birds with the Uniform Act

The public's concern over marijuana, whatever its actual extent, clearly exceeded its interest in any other aspect of the drug problem. Sometime late in 1934 the Bureau of Narcotics seems to have hit upon a golden solution to two of its most urgent problems: pressure for action on marijuana, against which the Bureau believed it could not move, and the states' slowness to adopt the Uniform Narcotic Drug Act, in which the states showed little interest. Fear of marijuana, Bureau leadership concluded, could be harnessed to propel the uniform act through the state legislatures. The act could in turn be displayed as proof of strong action against marijuana.

A uniform narcotic drug act had been drafted as early as 1918 by the American Medical Association and other professional associations, taken up in the 1920s by the Conference of Commissioners on Uniform State Laws, and allowed to languish through several later drafts. Upon entering office, Commissioner Anslinger had taken up a uniform law as a solution not only to inconsistencies and inadequacies in existing state laws, but also to what he considered a near total abdication of responsibility for narcotic enforcement on the states' part. A Bureau memorandum on the uniform act argued that prior to the Harrison Act, the states had made a "real effort" to enforce their own narcotic laws, "however ill-advised."[28]

The act was designed to remedy many of the often-cited causes for state inaction and to regulate activities simply beyond the Bureau's jurisdiction or the practical scope of its actions. These activities included simple possession, small-time dealing, and the problem of addicted physicians, who were sheltered by the "indifferent attitude on the part of the Medical Board of the States, the members of which are, of course, brother physicians." Stronger state laws would also provide an alternative when in "certain jurisdictions the National Government is faced with the predicament of having a Judge of the Federal Court who will sentence persistent violators" to only minimum terms.[29]

Commissioner Anslinger subsequently took particular satisfaction in Section 19 of the Uniform Narcotic Drug Act (UNDA), which required all state and local enforcement officers to cooperate fully with federal officers—cooperation that had been made mandatory for the Bureau by its charter act. A Bureau survey suggested that, beyond specific shortcomings in the states' drug laws, lack of uniformity hindered federal efforts to shift greater responsibility for enforcement to the states. As a consequence, the Bureau began cooperating with the National Conference of Commissioners on Uniform State Laws to draft a uniform act. Because the Bureau clearly understood that state deficiencies reflected indifference quite as much as inadequate laws or enforcement mechanisms, it seems remarkable that the commissioner placed so much faith in the ability of yet another law to invigorate state efforts. The uniform act, however, was embraced and promoted by the Bureau, working as it seemed to Anslinger in 1935, "alone . . . at least until very recently."[30]

The fifth draft was finally adopted in October of 1932 after intensive negotiations between the Bureau and interested professional associations. From the Bureau's point of view, it was far from ideal. It omitted provision for compulsory commitment and treatment of addicts and revocation by the courts of the licenses of convicted professionals, and provided only an optional clause by which marijuana might be controlled under the act. Nevertheless, the Bureau took up the UNDA as the best act obtainable and began an energetic campaign for its adoption.

A circular addressed to the governor of Colorado in January of 1933 urging adoption of the UNDA stressed the absence of impositions on the states. The act provided for "a minimum degree of limitation" on the legitimate trade; enactment would not block retention of desirable state laws not in conflict. "I wish to emphasize," the commissioner said, "that the enactment of the uniform narcotic law does not involve additional expense on the part of the State and therefore entails no addition to the present State budget." Enforcement could be charged to an existing state agency.[31] On the eve of Roosevelt's inauguration, as the nation awaited economic revival, this appeal was well-calculated. It was hardly consistent, however, with the Bureau's intention to increase state enforcement. Given the preoccupation with economic collapse and the submission of the act on the very eve of many states' legislative sessions, it was not surprising that only seven states enacted it by the end of 1934.

The Campaign for the Uniform Act in Colorado

The strategy of promoting the UNDA by appealing to fear of marijuana may have been suggested by a spectacularly gruesome axe murder in Florida, attributed at the time to marijuana and later credited with having brought about one of the first adoptions of the UNDA there. The suggested date for the adoption of this strategy, late 1934, corresponds with the Bureau of Narcotics' increased emphasis on marijuana and attention to the proposed uniform act, previously ignored. In November a special agent of the Bureau of Narcotics, Isabelle A. O'Neill, had come to Colorado on one of a series of carefully prepared visits to promote the act. The *Denver Post* reported the event with a yawn in a small, two-column-inch item blandly captioned "New Law Urged for Colorado."[32]

Nevertheless, several days later both major Denver newspapers carried editorials calling for adoption of the uniform act to suppress marijuana. The extent of the danger had been revealed in the recent series of raids throughout the nation, Agent Manning reported. Special efforts were essential to protect schoolchildren from the degeneracy and insanity caused by marijuana. The *Post* carried Manning's warning to young people of the drug's effects. That same month the *Rocky Mountain News* discovered that marijuana was growing wild in Denver's front yards. Several years later the *Post* commented that the uniform act had been passed and a special narcotics section created in the State Department of Health in an attempt "to combat the spread of the marijuana plague," an evil which "Colorado's legislature was forced to recognize . . . ." Dr. Roy L. Cleere, executive secretary of the State Board of Health when enforcement of the narcotic laws was assigned to the board, later recalled that the marijuana issue had drawn considerable attention to the campaign for the act's adoption.[33]

The Bureau prepared for the passage of the uniform act in Colorado with some care. The outgoing president of the National Association of Retail Druggists (NARD), a Coloradan, received a letter of thanks for his "excellent spirit of cooperation" at the last NARD convention. The Bureau sent along a copy of the act and arguments in its favor, which the druggist promised to bring to the attention of the Colorado Pharmacal Association's officers. The NARD was presumably one of "certain organizations" referred to by the U.S. Public Health Service's Dr. Walter Treadway which, "unless they are in accord, can balk any legislation submitted to a state legislature . . . ." Agent Manning prudently requested and received twenty-five copies of the act to be given to persons "interested in the enforcement of narcotic laws, in an effort to have them brought before the various State Legislatures."[34]

O'Neill's visit was meant to generate administrative support for the act. Governor Johnson could report to Commissioner Anslinger that he had "called particular attention to the subject of drugs" and the uniform act and that there was "little doubt but what something substantial will be passed and made the law of the State." Anslinger asked Manning to make his "best efforts" for the act in Colorado, but "without incurring any criticism for the so-called 'federal interference' . . . ." Reminding Manning that "an intensive and concentrated drive is being waged through the country," he urged him to contact the local affiliates of state and national organizations, whose constituents should be asked to write their senators.[35]

Manning reported that he had assurances of cooperation from the editors of Denver's newspapers and reporters of his acquaintance. Favorable editorials had appeared in both the *News* and the *Post* since the bill's introduction in January. Because the *News* editorial of February 4, 1935, directly followed a visit from Manning, its garbled contents are of some interest. "Conflict between the federal and state statutes has greatly interfered with efforts to stamp out the drug traffic," observed the *News*. "For example there is no Colorado statute governing marijuana, in consequence, that dangerous plant presents a constant menace." Not just sale or possession, but cultivation should be illegal. Passage of the uniform drug act was essential to control marijuana and would be of "aid to the federal government in its fight against the dope traffic."[36]

Colorado, in fact, had regulated the cultivation of marijuana since 1917. Second conviction for any contact with marijuana without a prescription had been a felony since 1929. It is difficult to know to which "conflicts" the editorial might have been referring, but it is clear that the agent's visit had reinforced the editor's conviction that narcotic control was primarily a federal responsibility. Manning was confident of the uniform law's easy passage in all the states of his district. One indication of the thoroughness of the Bureau's campaign was a letter, written three years later, offering the services of the Loveland, Colorado, Nature Study Club in the fight against marijuana. The writer asked if "Colorado has done as requested, and if not if he [Anslinger] still wants such action requested by the people or clubs."[37]

In preparing for the act's passage, Agent Manning worked closely with Congressman T. E. Childers, a Durango osteopath and chairman of the House Medical Affairs and Public Health Committee whom Manning later identified as the bill's "real sponsor." Manning was at pains to see that repeal of conflicting legislation did not eliminate Colorado's control of peyote as well as commitment and treatment of addicts, for both of which the uniform act made no provision. Although Manning foresaw no opposition, still he advised Anslinger, "I am and have been somewhat afraid that if I do not keep right on it, it may become sidetracked." There is no better indication of the share of the initiative Manning carried than his report of an invitation to explain the bill to a Senate committee. Manning had been invited because the "Committee was so busy that it did not have time to read the bill."[38]

Colorado was not alone in dealing haphazardly with the proposed uniform act. Wyoming's bill had been lost after being introduced in the last-minute rush of an unexpectedly early adjournment. The bill had begun to lag in Utah. The status of "our Uniform Law" in New Mexico was unknown. In Arizona the uniform law had been botched by amendments, and passage had become thoroughly bogged down. Manning observed, "I have found that if one does not get behind these bills and stay with them, that there will not be much done about it." The proposed Arizona bill is an extreme example of combined Bureau initiative and state haphazardness, having provided milder penalties for the second offense than for the first.[39]

Colorado's bill incorporating relatively moderate penalties proceeded uneventfully through both houses and received the governor's signature on March 16, 1937. By the end of the month, Manning could report with satisfaction that New Mexico, Utah, and Arizona had also passed a uniform act, and all included the provision for controlling the growth, production, sale, and use of cannabis. If Washington could supply him with a copy of regulations developed by a state which had already adopted the uniform act, he would be prepared to supply them if asked, and implementation could be obtained in the near future. Manning was also careful to forward to Commissioner Anslinger a list of those officials, legislators, and private citizens to whom credit for the passage of the bill was due. The suggested letters of appreciation were promptly sent. Manning singled out Paul J. Stodghill, a Denver pharmacist who had met with Anslinger in New Orleans and had subsequently been active on behalf of the act.[40]

The Uniform Act Reinforces Dependence on the Bureau

Less than a month after its passage, Governor Johnson received a request from the Bureau for "an expression of opinion of what the Uniform Narcotic Drug Act has achieved in your state." "We understand that this law is primarily designed to make our state law conform to the Federal Narcotic Law and the laws of other states," replied the governor, "... and we intend to cooperate fully with the Federal Bureau of Narcotics." The governor's reply conveys the clear impression that, in adopting the law and standing ready to cooperate with federal officials, state officials had discharged their responsibilities. This impression is strengthened by the state's subsequent, and ultimately rather comic, quest for implementation regulations.[41]

In early May Manning forwarded a request by Colorado State Board of Health officials for a rough draft of regulations prepared by the Bureau's Law Division. "In a way," Manning explained, "they look upon this Uniform Narcotic Law as our law; that we are responsible for its passage and they feel we should assist in putting it into force, which cannot be done until the necessary rules and regulations are promulgated." Manning was brusquely advised that federal precedent should be adequate, that no state had needed printed regulations, and that endorsing any regulations would be "an unwarranted interference" by federal officials. As for implementing the newly enacted regulation of marijuana, the Bureau was "not aware that any satisfactory and effective method [had] been devised by any of the states."[42]

Nearly a year later the acting secretary of the State Board of Health, Dr. M. F. Haralson, trumped the Bureau's refusal to supply regulations. Addressing Anslinger as "Dear Harry," Haralson pleaded his utter inability to provide regulations without the assistance of his old friend. Anslinger, cornered and still protesting the novelty of the request, responded with suggestions and closed with the assurance that if Haralson should require further assistance, "you have but to ask for it."[43]

The Uniform Narcotic Drug Act was, indeed, the Bureau's act, the text supplied by its agents and its passage insured by their assiduous lobbying and hard work with the press. Adoption was secured on the one hand by fanning fears of marijuana, and on the other by assuring the states that its enforcement would change and cost nothing. The course of the act's adoption demonstrated that, whatever the actual state of illicit drug use, the public was generally unaware and unconcerned unless prodded. Only by the most unrelenting efforts was the Denver regional office able to fan the ember of public concern into flame long enough to fuel the act's passage. Ultimately, pursuit of the uniform act did not reinvigorate state commitment to enforcement against users and small-time dealers. The Bureau instead had reinforced the belief that all illicit drug use was primarily the responsibility of the federal government.

Chapter Five

Colorado and the Marijuana Tax Act

THE FAILURE of prohibition prompted only a few critics to argue for reconsideration of controlling other drugs. They argued that the structure of enforcement based on the Harrison Act had aggravated drug misuse, just as the Nineteenth Amendment and Volstead Act had aggravated misuse of alcohol. These critics went unheard, scarcely attracting even a rebuttal. In effect, the Bureau of Narcotics asserted that prohibition of illicit drugs would be different—because alcohol and nicotine, favored by the majority, were simply not drugs at all. Prohibition's expensive lessons were forgotten as the New Deal extended federal responsibility for social welfare and law enforcement.

The Bureau Embraces a Federal Marijuana Act

The campaign for a federal marijuana law, far more than the new Uniform Narcotic Drug Act, reaffirmed the Bureau's commitment to strict prohibition of dangerous drugs. The campaign also required the reversal of the Bureau's long-standing marijuana policy. Since the Harrison Act's passage in 1914, the Bureau and its predecessors had routinely deflected pressure for federal action against marijuana. Marijuana, they protested, was essentially a local problem. A fundamental shift in the division of responsibilities between federal and state governments underlay the Bureau's reversal. In Colorado the Bureau's campaign for the Marijuana Tax Act (MTA) fanned fears of marijuana, which led Colorado to increase sharply its own marijuana penalties. Perversely, the MTA's passage prompted Colorado to abandon responsibility for marijuana enforcement. Why did the Bureau abandon its opposition to federal control of marijuana?

The Bureau had insisted repeatedly and as late as 1937, the year of the federal marijuana act, that marijuana was rarely smuggled from abroad or across state lines. An import ban would therefore be pointless. "Marihuana," a Bureau official observed, "is not generally handled by well organized distributing syndicates." As a local problem, marijuana was beyond the reach of federal authority under the interstate commerce clause. The proper remedy was local legislation, readily enacted "overnight." The Bureau discreetly but vigorously rebuffed proposals for federal control based on the power of taxation. Taxing marijuana would endanger the extended interpretation of the Harrison Act, upheld by the courts only upon a narrowly defined use of the taxation power.[1]

New Deal legislation, however, was committing the federal government to a broad range of social and economic reforms, and narrow constitutional interpretation was in retreat. The extension of federal involvement with crime begun by Hoover's Wickersham Commission produced a spate of anti-crime legislation early in Roosevelt's first term. The highest volume of new criminal law came in 1934, when Congress adopted almost the entire Roosevelt crime program. The Interstate Commission on Crime, established in 1935, aptly summarized the shift: "The past six years have witnessed the greatest extension of federal criminal law in the history of our country. Matters heretofore committed entirely to the states and municipalities have suddenly been brought within the compass of federal jurisdiction."[2] After the Supreme Court had sustained federal authority over kidnaping, fugitives, stolen property, and firearms, the Bureau abandoned its reluctance to attack marijuana.

Late in 1935 Commissioner Anslinger approved preparation of a bill for federal control of marijuana. The Bureau now argued that state indifference or inability to control marijuana made federal control imperative. Anslinger had repeatedly insisted that the states must assume their share of responsibility for controlling drugs in partnership with federal authorities. He adamantly denied that the Bureau had promoted the uniform act to "pass the buck" to the states. Earlier in 1935 he had opposed a federal marijuana law, arguing instead for the optional marijuana provision of the uniform act: "If the states will go along with that, then the federal government ought to step in and coordinate the work, but until the states become conscious of their own problem, I think it is a mistake for the federal government to take on the whole job." By the end of 1935, twenty-seven states had adopted the uniform act, most with the marijuana provision included. Although publicly optimistic, Bureau officials knew that the states had generally assigned a low priority to enforcement of their own narcotic laws, which had varied widely in their provisions and effectiveness.[3]

The Bureau's decision to seek a federal marijuana law came before the UNDA could have a fair trial. It was early apparent, however, that the states were unenthusiastic about enforcing the uniform act, commonly perceived as the Bureau's creation. State authorities considered the act's passage a favor to federal authorities, assisting them in *their* enforcement activity. State licensing boards continued to defer action against all but a handful of the professionals recommended by the Bureau for sanctions. The Bureau had in fact worked hard to invigorate local enforcement of drug laws. As late as 1937 it reprinted with approval the report of the Committee on Drug Addiction of the Conference of State and Provincial Health Officials, which stressed in elementary terms that *all* state, county, and city officials, not just the boards of professional examiners, were responsible for drug law enforcement.[4]

Testifying for the federal marijuana act, however, Commissioner Anslinger argued that simple indifference explained the states' efforts to enforce their own marijuana laws. He considered Colorado one of only four states to have made a serious effort. Colorado had charged the Board of Health's Division of Food and Drugs with enforcement of the uniform act and specifically with preventing "the cultivation and the distribution of marijuana." Even in Colorado and the three other enforcing states, Anslinger argued, a federal act would allow the Bureau to assist with additional manpower and money.[5] But a contemporary study concluded that the Federal Bureau of Investigation's comparable efforts to improve state and local law enforcement had instead promoted the agency's own image as "a symbol of efficiency in general criminal-law enforcement . . . ." The study's director concluded that "Federal activity tends to divert attention from urgent situations in state and local governments; and the current interest in federal activity seems to be largely concentrated on one or two well-advertised agencies."[6] The FBI was clearly one of those agencies. The Bureau of Narcotics was, in all probability, the other. Its annual *Traffic in Narcotics and Dangerous Drugs*, for example, brimmed with spectacular accounts of arrests and seizures.

The Bureau Finds an Opportunity in Marijuana

The receding danger of undermining the Harrison Act, coupled with apathetic state enforcement, brought the Bureau to see in marijuana control not a pitfall but an opportunity. Fear of marijuana, aroused to insure passage of the Uniform Narcotic Drug Act, had easily outlived interest in the act. From the outset, Bureau chiefs had faced a dilemma. On one hand they felt compelled to demonstrate that the Bureau was effective in suppressing illicit drugs and that "the present policies of the United States government are materially discouraging drug addiction." The Bureau regularly reported that rates of use had fallen, when in fact the reported rates fluctuated considerably. Increases in adulteration, diversion from legitimate channels, thefts, and higher prices were all read as signs that supplies and use were drying up or that "light," easily cured habits were becoming more common.[7]

In the lean 1930s, scrambling for appropriations amidst a pack of new agencies and programs, the Bureau capitalized on public fears of crime. Bureau reports hammered at the criminality of those "put away" on drug charges, stressing that many had "some of the worst criminal records in the United States for major crimes."[8] Bureau statistics, however, show that violent crimes were quite uncommon among those convicted of drug law violations. Victimless crimes and theft account for all but a few offenses in these supposed careers of major crime.

Regular reports of work well done and a problem nearly solved might demonstrate the Bureau's effectiveness. They would not build public support for a broader role and an increased budget. Marijuana, on the other hand, could be presented as a grave, and more importantly, a new threat. The Bureau could promote itself as a champion against marijuana without fear of criticism for prior laxness in discharging its responsibilities. Commissioner Anslinger clearly believed he was fighting organized crime's move into illicit drugs after the repeal of prohibition. Neither the commissioner nor the Bureau, however, argued that organized crime was behind the rising use of marijuana. Indeed, anti-narcotic publicists, both in and out of the Bureau's favor, argued as late as

1937 that marijuana traffic was usually local and an individual affair.[9]

Marijuana touched the public's fear of crime, but not because organized crime trafficked in it or its price drove addicts to crime. Rather, many believed that marijuana itself incited users to violence, a view vividly presented in the Bureau-inspired commercial film, *Reefer Madness*. Despite an admitted lack of previous figures, the Bureau in 1935 reported "a dangerous and rapidly increasing traffic in cannabis." Prior to the federal marijuana act, these statistics could only have been supplied by the states. The Census Bureau, however, found contemporary state figures on crime and law enforcement so fragmentary and variable as to be virtually worthless. Indeed, one researcher found them inadequate to determine even "whether crime is increasing or decreasing."[10]

The Bureau's use of both reassurance and alarm was evident in the *Denver Post* on the eve of the federal marijuana bill's introduction in January of 1937. "Uniform State Dope Law Has Aided Colorado," read the *Post*'s caption, "Traffic Almost Stamped Out, Declares US Bureau Chief." Harry D. Smith, the Bureau's district supervisor, cited the act as a "powerful weapon in the hands of federal and state authorities," facilitating "whole-hearted" cooperation. In little more than a year, the act had been a near total success. Smith also reported progress on marijuana, "one of the main problems being confronted in this district."[11] The Bureau had done a superb job—but a new menace had reared its head.

Marijuana was particularly resistant to accurate statistical assessment. Other drugs were typically found as a refined product of measurable degrees of purity. But cannabis virtually defied measurement. It might be encountered as hashish (the extracted resin), as "reefer" cigarettes, or in bulk (dried, green, even growing in the field)—all with widely varying potency. A Bureau request that officers report enforcement activity against marijuana "whenever they read about or hear of any purchase or seizure of cannabis," although only after confirmation, suggests the unreliability of these statistics. The Bureau reported that in 1936 Colorado ranked fifth—behind California, Ohio, Louisiana, and Illinois—in the number of seizures of cannabis. This ranking is of particular interest, because for the two preceding years Colorado's Legislative Reference office had told the Bureau that such enforcement figures did not exist, had never been collected, and would be "impossible" to obtain.[12]

The "Weed of Insanity and Death" Campaign

Many years later Commissioner Anslinger succinctly described the role he and the Bureau of Narcotics played in raising the public's awareness of marijuana:

> As the marijuana situation grew worse, I knew action had to be taken to get proper control legislation passed. By 1937, under my direction, the Bureau launched two important steps. First a legislative plan to seek from Congress a new law that would place marijuana and its distribution directly under federal control. Second, on radio and at major forums, such as that presented annually by the New York *Herald Tribune*, I told the story of this evil weed of the fields and river beds and roadsides. I wrote articles for magazines; our agents gave hundreds of lectures to parents, educators, social and civic leaders. In network broadcasts I reported on the growing list of crimes including murder and rape. I described the nature of marijuana and its close kinship to hashish. I continued to hammer at the facts. I believe we did a thorough job, for the public was alerted, and the laws to protect them were passed, both nationally and at the state level.[13]

Substantiating the commissioner's account of his efforts, Bureau files bulged with drafts of speeches to professional and civic organizations, letters from concerned citizens responding to the commissioner's appeals for action, references to broadcasts and public speeches, and articles and editorials inspired by narcotics agents and submitted to the Bureau. A letter to Anslinger from Ken Clark, chief correspondent of Universal Services, reflected the origin and results of many of these published pieces. "Dear Harry," wrote Clark, "Am still hearing about that Sunday feature I wrote about marijuana. Enclosed is another letter." The letter, from Alfa F. Ostrander, secretary of the Department of Publication at Colorado State Teachers College, asked for more information and proposed to enlist the Greeley Business and Professional Women's Club and the State Federation of Business and Professional Women in the fight against marijuana. Ostrander had responded to Clark's article, "Murders Due to Marihuana Sweeping U.S.," which warned that a "hideous monster was amuck in the land."[14]

Material appearing under Anslinger's own name was no more restrained. A month before Congress took action on the marijuana bill, the July 1937 *American Magazine* carried "Marihuana: Assassin of Youth," co-authored by Anslinger and sensational crime writer Courtney Ryley Cooper. Marijuana was "contributing to our alarming wave of sex crimes, according to many public officials." Because of the states' "official ignorance of its effect," marijuana flourished unimpeded. Although all but one of the states had anti-marijuana laws, in the absence of a federal law, "the powerful right arm which could support these states has been all but impotent." This was about to be remedied. Far from a relaxation of efforts, however, Anslinger and Cooper called for "campaigns of education in every school" to tell "the insanity, the disgrace, the horror."[15]

The Bureau's campaign was on the scale Anslinger remembered, although it dated from 1935 rather than 1937. But it seems to have created a diffuse, patchy, and often muddled concern with marijuana rather than an articulate public demand for federal action. After brief hearings, the Marijuana Tax Act passed in August of 1937. The Bureau's publicity campaign may have helped beat down scattered opposition from the medical profession. Most congressmen, however, apparently had little idea of what marijuana was and simply voted for an extension of federal control over narcotics as recommended by the Bureau.

Congress would in all likelihood have approved the Marijuana Tax Act without the Bureau's publicity campaign. A week later, the MTA's passage drew only a two-sentence mention in the *New York Times*, hardly indicating an aroused public. Neither can the laboriously produced expressions of public concern be read as "further evidence that the problem is a serious one," as the Bureau and its advocates did repeatedly. In Denver, Agent Smith promptly announced a "war to the finish" on marijuana, but the act was otherwise little remarked. Frederick T. Merrill, a national anti-marijuana crusader, cited as evidence of the marijuana threat the "concentrated efforts within the various states to enact preventive legislation," appeals for help from civic organizations, and "publicity drives against marihuana abuse" by many newspapers, "notably the Denver News, the Minneapolis Star, and the Chattanooga News." He chose to ignore clear evidence that the expressions of concern were solicited by Bureau officials and buttressed by the Bureau's repeated assurances that the problem was indeed grave.[16]

The Marijuana Campaign Brings a Response in Colorado

Most immediately, the campaign prompted the passage of considerably stiffer state and local laws. In Colorado the campaign for the federal marijuana act can be traced with exceptional clarity. Following the Uniform Narcotic Drug Act's passage and reports of success in curbing drug use, Colorado's interest in marijuana and dope had languished. Drug stories in the Denver press were as likely to describe a Hollywood star's narcotics habit or the seizure of a fortune in drugs aboard a Pacific steamer as to report a local arrest for marijuana possession or sale. Nevertheless, the campaign for a federal anti-marijuana law reawakened fears. In November of 1936 the Rotary Club and Junior Chamber of Commerce of Alamosa adopted resolutions citing marijuana's "menace to public health and safety" and asserting that "State and United States Statutes are not effective enough." They warned that cultivation was increasing, especially in the San Luis Valley surrounding Alamosa, where many residents were Hispanic. Given the presumed urgency, it was curious that two months passed before the Bureau's copy was mailed. The Bureau replied that a federal act was already in the works.[17]

Alamosa's expression of concern bore fruit more directly. In January of 1937 Congressman Frank R. Divers of Alamosa and Costilla counties introduced in the Colorado legislature a bill to increase drastically the penalties for growing, selling, or giving away marijuana. The bill proposed to make all violations felonies and to raise the penalties for first, second, and subsequent offenses alike to one to ten years in the state penitentiary. The bill attracted nineteen bipartisan cosponsors, representing a pyramid of counties broadly based on Colorado's southern tier of "Spanish" counties and tapering northward to include the state's major urban concentrations in Pueblo and Denver. In the Senate, members from Denver and Pueblo counties sponsored the measure. Passage in both houses was uneventful, and the bill received final approval on April 15. Agent Smith was pleased to forward a copy to Washington, citing it as a clear indication that Colorado had been aroused to the peril of marijuana. By amending the UNDA-based state law to increase penalties, he concluded, Colorado had taken effective action.[18]

Unfortunately, Congressman Divers' bill as written had amended the act of 1929, not the UNDA-based bill passed by the Colorado legislature six years later. That 1935 act, the Washington office pointed out to a chagrined Agent Smith, had repealed most existing drug legislation, including the act of 1929. Smith made hurried inquiries, confirmed Washington's reading of the act, and concluded that "the newly enacted statute means nothing whatever." Smith was quick to point out that Divers had never consulted the district office, or the state attorney general, or anyone knowledgeable on the subject. Divers was now the object of considerable criticism, he said, particularly from his cosponsors.[19] Efforts to correct the oversight suggested the shallowness of concern with marijuana. A gloss in the session's laws indicated that the 1929 act had subsequently been amended—but in fact it had been repealed.

Following passage of Colorado's marijuana penalties act in mid-April, the State Board of Health announced in early May a combined city and state marijuana drive. Nevertheless, until August the press paid only sporadic attention to marijuana. Interest intensified in the fall but had largely dissipated by year's end. Enforcement activity, as always, was a great deal easier to report than actual drug use, which would have required time-consuming investigation. The *Post* did its best to enliven creation of the new Division of Food and Drugs under the State Board of Health. "Colorado Department Waging Winning Fight Upon Marijuana," read the *Post*'s caption, "New Agency Battles to Destroy Narcotic that Leads to Eventual Insanity After Making Beasts of Its Victims." The work of Dr. Roy L. Cleere, secretary of the State Board of Health, Walter Lear, commissioner of Food and Drugs, and A. D. Catterson, Jr., chief narcotic officer, had led to the discovery of six marijuana patches and five convictions—all without federal assistance, the *Post* proudly reported. An accompanying syndicated article sketched a lurid picture of marijuana as "the Dynamite that Blasts Souls."[20]

Several days later the *Denver News* began a series on marijuana, stressing the uncontrolled danger of the "American Hasheesh," which, far from being under control, was still available to schoolchildren. Not surprisingly, that summer the *News* traced the root of the state's marijuana problem to the absence of a federal law. "When sellers of the drug are arrested they usually are prosecuted under the vagrancy ordinance and fined a maximum of $300," said the *News*. "There is a state law under which persons found with the weed in their possession can be tried, but it is seldom used. Evidence sufficient to prosecute is hard to get." The *News* duly reported federal agents' conclusion that the single greatest factor in the spreading use of marijuana was the lack of a federal law. Fortunately, the *News* reassured its readers, the Bureau of Narcotics, armed with a new federal act passed only days earlier, was preparing for an "open season" on marijuana on October 1.

The *News* story, locally researched, offered a picture of marijuana use remarkably different from the specter of madness and mayhem most often sketched by the Bureau. Little was known of the drug medically, said the *News*. Beet workers returning from the fields brought with them sacks of marijuana "which augments their scanty income." Police officers believed that, in combination with alcohol, marijuana produced sex crimes and "a state of maniacal violence." Nevertheless, the drug was so cheaply available that "its devotees do not have to resort to major crime to buy it." Unlike the narcotics user, "marijuana users seem normal to the uninformed." "It is," the report concluded, "a poor man's drug used as an escape from harsh reality," from which children should be protected, even if adult use could not be controlled. Throughout the remainder of August, Denver's two dailies competed in revealing the extent of marijuana use in Denver, handing leads to the police and covering raids on marijuana "farms." Colorado's efforts were sufficiently vigorous that enforcement officials in neighboring states wrote the State Board of Health for information.[21]

Press interest slackened after the Board of Health abandoned its campaign against growers. The board had been denied firearms for its inspectors, the only unarmed members of city and county raiding parties. The State Executive Council had balked at appropriating $102.75 for the purchase of three revolvers, explaining that "We don't want any standing armies in this state." The press could only look forward to the renewed attack on marijuana in October, when the federal act became effective and federal assistance available.[22]

Those who looked to Colorado for guidance in a brisk application of the new federal law were not disappointed. One week to the day after the Marijuana Tax Act took effect, federal judge J. Foster Symes sentenced one Denver man to four years and a $1,000 fine and another to eighteen months. "I consider marijuana the worst of all narcotics—far worse than the use of morphine or cocaine," said Judge Symes. Commissioner Anslinger agreed wholeheartedly with Symes and came to Denver for the sentencing, the first anywhere under the new act. He lavished praise on the U.S. district attorneys who had brought the case: "These men," said Anslinger, "have shown the way to other district attorneys throughout the nation."

Unfortunately, they had. Federal power would now be applied to sweeping up small dealers and marijuana users. Samuel R. Caldwell, fifty-eight years of age, and Moses Baca, twenty-six, had been arrested on Wednesday, October 6, after agents, by chance, had broken up a street sale. Indicted on Thursday, they were convicted and sentenced on Friday. The two men received Judge Symes' exemplary penalties instead of the usual sixty-day maximum provided by the city and state laws under which they would previously have been prosecuted. In sentencing Baca, who was reported to have said that using marijuana for six years had made him "a wild beast," Symes voiced his hope that "eighteen months in the penitentiary will cure you." Expressing his thanks, Commissioner Anslinger reversed the argument that the Marijuana Tax Act would allow the Bureau to assist state and local authorities struggling against marijuana. The commissioner gratefully noted "the full cooperation of the police," without whom "our hands would be tied."[23]

Weakening Local Responsibility

Anslinger's grateful observation on the relation of federal and local authorities was indeed prophetic. Medical uses of cannabis, never extensive, virtually disappeared after the MTA's passage, making superfluous the act's elaborate provisions for regulating legitimate traffic. Possession and all nonmedical transfers simply became federal crimes. Overlapping jurisdictions over marijuana repeated the experience of prohibition. Records of marijuana seizures by state and local authorities before and after the passage of the MTA demonstrate the lesson unmistakably. State and local authorities abdicated responsibility to federal agencies.

The 1938–39 report of the Colorado State Board of Health reflects this division of labor, listing among the objectives of its Food and Drug Division, "to aid the Federal narcotic bureau in the control of narcotics, including marijuana." The Food and Drug Division concerned itself with regulating the legitimate trade and preventing marijuana cultivation. For the most part it simply cooperated with the Bureau of Narcotics in bringing criminal cases.[24] That the Bureau promoted this transfer of responsibility is evident in correspondence between the secretary of the State Board of Health and Elizabeth Bass, supervisor of District 13, headquartered in Denver, and subsequently between Bass and Anslinger.

Bass found fault with a certain state food and drug inspector, "a perfectly ignorant person, fat and unintelligent," who had, among other things, presumed "to assume functions that belong only to the Bureau of Narcotics in the matter of investigating violations of the Harrison Narcotic Drug Act *and the Uniform Narcotic Act of Colorado* . . ." (emphasis added). Bass had warned the Board of Health that the inspector should not address an assembly of women's clubs, as she was "sure the Bureau of Narcotics would object to his talking on that subject."[25] Bass was a political appointee with a substantial record as a crusader for reform, and she undoubtedly exhibited a degree of independence and candor unusual in a career civil servant. She did not, however, misrepresent the Bureau's views.

After passage of the Marijuana Tax Act, the urgency faded rapidly from the commissioner's and the Bureau's pronouncements on marijuana. Suppression of marijuana was now charged to the Bureau, which might be held accountable. The Bureau, moreover, was obliged to counter the charge that its educational campaign had introduced the drug to children previously unaware of it. The Narcotics Section of the Interstate Crime Commission warned of "the danger involved in a campaign which is over-emphatic, which paints a lurid or romantic picture of 'reefer' smoking, or which may give children the idea that here is a new 'thrill,' a modern experience." The Bureau's assistant commissioner now cautioned an inquirer that "the drug is not used by youth so generally as might be inferred from some rather hysterical statements which have appeared on the subject in various parts of the country." He urged that any warnings should employ great discretion "to avoid arousing unhealthy curiosity in the minds of children."[26]

Commissioner Anslinger himself, who had called less than a year before for campaigns of education in every school to tell "the insanity, the disgrace, the horror of marijuana," turned suddenly reticent. To a West

Virginia woman requesting guidance, he curtly replied that the Bureau had no suggestions to offer. Rather, "the parent and teacher are the logical ones to direct educational programs." The Bureau later cut off a self-styled religious anti-marijuana crusader whose pretentious inquiries had been answered meticulously prior to the MTA. The Bureau cited "inaccuracies" in his material—most of it culled from Bureau publications. Anslinger himself still preached the original message from time to time, usually to adults. His article for the Missouri Peace Officers Association in 1941, "Marihuana: The Assassin of the Human Mind," salvaged much of "Marihuana: Assassin of Youth." The 1941 article omitted the dangers to youth of marijuana, "a more terrible enemy to society than a mad dog," in favor of stressing that "Marihuana is destroying so much of the manhood of the race." The problem, he informed the officers, had been to develop "a technique that would *restrict rather than extend a knowledge of the effects of the drug* on the human system" (emphasis added). "By a process of trial and error," the commissioner continued, "it was found that the surest way to terminate the use of marihuana was to exterminate the weed wherever it grows." Clearly, a public aroused at the wrong time and against the wrong drug could be a major liability.[27]

The Colorado press, without further stimulus from the Bureau or new legislation, fed its readers only a thin diet of stories detailing enforcement by state and federal officials in Colorado and elsewhere. Now and again the operation of a "dope ring" or a peyote story received cursory treatment. Typical were Supervisor Smith's revelation in 1937 of "one of the most vicious dope rings" of recent years and the arrest of fifteen suspects in "the most sinister dope ring ever to operate in Colorado" in 1941. Public attention, however, was increasingly engaged by the war looming in Europe and the Pacific. The war itself disrupted the long supply lines bringing opiates from the Middle East and Central and Southeast Asia to Europe and North America. Addicts were forced to extreme expedients, even to taking a cure, said Supervisor Bass, but not to marijuana. Marijuana was no substitute "for the powerful drugs of the poppy."[28]

As the burden of marijuana cases shifted to federal authorities, arrests in Denver for violation of city drug ordinances dropped abruptly from seventy-one in 1937 to nineteen in 1938, the year after the MTA's passage. Arrests continued to decline slowly, averaging just over five per year during America's involvement in the Second World War. In 1944 Colorado made its first attempt at a full report to the Bureau of enforcement activity. Most of the district attorneys who replied reported little or no activity. Those not replying, said the assistant attorney general, might be interpreted as "no prosecutions." Colorado reported a total of twenty-two narcotic violations and fifteen marijuana violations. "Almost without exception," wrote the assistant attorney general, "we are advised that, where narcotic violations were found, the matter was referred to the federal authorities and that local officers did nothing but gather what evidence they could for submission to the federal officers." It is difficult to imagine a more telling commentary on the Bureau's efforts to invigorate state action against illicit drugs.[29]

Chapter Six

Creating the Modern Drug Dilemma

EDUCTIONS in the supply of illicit drugs, particularly the opiates, might have explained the sharp fall in arrests during the Second World War, but might just as well have increased arrests as users turned to force or fraud to obtain drugs from legitimate sources. The enlistment of young men in their late teens and twenties, who made up a disproportionate share of those arrested for drug violations, probably contributed to the decline in arrests. The decline, however, was roughly proportionate in older age groups as well. Arrests most likely fell simply because public and official attention was redirected to more urgent concerns.

The Return of the Peacetime Drug Market

The Bureau of Narcotics, drawing on the experience of previous wars, expected post-war illicit drug use to soar. Enforcement officials sometimes cited wartime medical addictions or addictions acquired through contact with addicts abroad, but they primarily feared a boom in illicit supplies. Surplus military stocks of opiates might be stolen, but above all, peace would reopen traditional sources in Central and Southeast Asia. This resumed flow of East Asian opiates would join alternative supplies developed in Iran, India, and Mexico. High drug prices—produced by strict enforcement and the world's highest incomes—insured that the United States would be the market of choice for illicit suppliers.

In 1947 the Bureau reported the return of the drug traffic to "conditions of pre-war days," and in 1949 that there was "plenty [of heroin] available at most times."[1] The Bureau also detected a rising traffic in cocaine, believed insignificant since the early 1930s. The barbiturate sedatives, to which some opiate addicts had turned during the war, began to appear in the illicit trade. Marijuana smuggling had grown near war's end, possibly along routes developed for crude Mexican "brown" heroin. Seizures of imported marijuana continued to rise in the immediate post-war years, as did seizures of refined cannabis products such as hashish, previously little known in the United States. Colorado, however, escaped the new influx of drugs longer than states with large port cities.

The Post-War Response to Drugs in Colorado

Colorado's own enforcement efforts had continued to atrophy during the war years. In 1945 the Food and Drug Division listed cooperation with the Bureau of Narcotics against illicit drugs as "in addition" to its main activity in regulating the legitimate trade. Lack of personnel and inadequate salaries made even this routine regulation sporadic. The inadequacy was not specific to drug control. The Board of Health observed "how greatly this state has depended upon federal allotments for building the foundations of its essential public health programs." The end of wartime programs forced health officials to fall back on state appropriations averaging about $.10 per citizen per year, "among the lowest expended for such purposes by any state." The board did not even include drug control in its list of recommended projects. Drug use simply did not seem pressing until 1950.[2]

In the early post-war years, the Colorado legislature routinely adopted the Bureau's recommended revisions in state laws. Colorado responded reasonably promptly to revisions recommended by the Bureau's district agent in 1946. After considerable discussion with State Health Department officials and some hard bargaining with representatives of the Colorado Pharmacal Association and the Colorado Medical Society, the chief of the Bureau's Denver office had a package of amendments ready for presentation to the legislature in January of 1947.

The simplest change District Supervisor A. B. Crisler proposed was to control isonipecaine (Demerol), a synthetic morphine first produced in Germany during the war. The second proposed amendment would narrow the list of opiate preparations exempt from regulation, although the Bureau had earlier urged that only weak preparations of codeine be exempt. Wartime experience of addicts who sustained their habit on paregoric and cough syrups now heightened the Bureau's concern. Finally, the Bureau's agent recommended increasing penalties sharply to a maximum of $1,000 and five years in the state penitentiary.

Economics explained the call for stiffer penalties. Crisler had recommended the increase because prosecuting attorneys were being "denied prosecution for violations of this Act because first offenders, if convicted, would have to serve time in the county jail. County attorneys claim the county cannot afford to board the prisoners, nor are they properly equipped to handle addicts undergoing withdrawal of narcotics." If the offense were a felony, convicted violators could be unloaded on the state.[3]

The bill passed unopposed in the Senate, but Congressman Carlson, Speaker of the House and chairman of the Rules Committee, objected to the increased penalty for first offenders. The impasse was readily broken. As Agent Crisler later recalled: "After some clever political maneuvering by Mr. Glenn Myles, Chairman of the Colorado Pharmacal Association Legislative Committee, Representative Carlson assured us that he would not oppose the original Senate bill when it again reached the floor of the house."[4] Unfortunately, the bill signed by Governor Knous was the amended draft that Carlson had agreed to abandon, not the bill passed by the legislature. Crisler's successor reported that the state assistant attorney general had

> ... advised me to say nothing about the mistake until there is another meeting of the legislature. We can go on as we have been under the law signed by the Governor and it is doubtful whether it will become generally known that the amendment is null and void. If attacked in the courts, there is really no amendment and therefore no legislation governing the sale of isonipecaine or paregoric without prescription.

Enforcing an invalid act was the most palatable solution.[5]

When the legislature next met two years later, the Bureau's acting district supervisor, Terry Talent, took no chances. He had "solicited the assistance of the editors of the Post some time ago on this matter." The *Denver Post's* editorial repeated Bureau warnings that "Narcotic violations in this federal region" were on the rise. Significantly, the *Post* observed that the increase "may be related to Colorado's weak law," which limited first offense penalties to a maximum of $300 and six months in jail. The new bill, essentially identical to the one miscarried two years earlier, discreetly repealed the botched act of 1947. But while the new act defined four new drugs, it carelessly failed to control three of them.[6]

The Bureau's First Post-War Campaign

In 1948 and 1949 the Bureau had reported that the rate of addiction, after falling steadily since the Harrison Act of 1914, had again begun to rise. Most alarming to the Bureau was "an increase in the number of young persons, those in their teens and early twenties, arrested for violation of the Federal marijuana and narcotic laws in New York, Chicago and San Francisco." Especially disturbing was the "increasing number of these young narcotic offenders who admit starting the use of narcotics with marijuana, then after a short while changing to the more powerful narcotics such as heroin, morphine and cocaine."[7]

A research review published three years later, however, failed to support the Bureau's finding of a higher number of young opiate addicts. Arrests of marijuana users apparently made up a large share of the rise in drug arrests cited by the Bureau as proof that addiction rates were rising. Investigators had reviewed 159 studies of social and psychological factors in opiate addiction conducted since the comprehensive survey published by Terry and Pellens in 1928. The review stressed the difficulty of estimating either addiction rates or the number of addicts but reported a probable decline in the rate of addiction from eight to two per 10,000 since 1928. Still, the Bureau's assertion that the age of addiction was falling and the number of younger marijuana users rising came to be generally believed.[8]

The Bureau's assertion that marijuana "led" to opiates was meant to answer a growing volume of substantial marijuana studies published in the decade since the Marijuana Tax Act's passage in 1937. The studies undercut the Bureau's earlier claim that marijuana was "the worst of all narcotics," the cause of addiction, violence, insanity, and death. Dr. J. D. Reichard, recently head of the federal drug hospital at Lexington, Kentucky, was blunt in his assessment. Marijuana, Reichard reported in 1946, did not produce addiction, criminal behavior, juvenile delinquency, or mental illness. Best known was the 1944 study conducted for Mayor La Guardia of New York by the New York Academy of Medicine. The Bureau

vehemently rejected this study, which Anslinger subsequently characterized as "giddy sociology and medical mumbo-jumbo." Organized crime, he
asserted, had exploited the report to nurture public doubt, and this had
paid off with "extra millions in the pockets of the hoods."[9]

In its renewed effort to raise public concern, the Bureau employed
methods and contacts developed in its campaigns for the Uniform Narcotic Drug Act and the Marijuana Tax Act. Since the early 1920s, opponents of drug abuse had debated whether educational efforts and publicity discouraged would-be users or aroused unhealthy curiosity. After the
MTA's passage, the Bureau had adopted the position that "improper" publicity spread addiction. This posture now exposed independent opponents
of narcotics to criticism, reinforcing the Bureau's role as the sole source of
responsible information. The actions of the National Conference of the
Women's Christian Temperance Union, meeting in Denver in September
of 1950, demonstrated the success of this policy. Citing the Bureau's con-
tention that "material dramatizing the use of narcotic drugs" spread addiction, the conference resolved to oppose "the indiscriminate use of narcotic themes as presently exploited in motion pictures, radio and televi-
sion programs and certain types of magazines and newspaper articles."[10]

The Bureau, indeed, left little to chance in disseminating its views on
narcotics. "Numerous magazine articles and newspaper stories appeared
in 1951," the Bureau reported, and "most of these articles were prepared
[by the Bureau] at the request of publishers desirous of meeting a growing public interest in the subject matter." The Bureau characterized two
of these articles, including one credited to Anslinger, as "accurate and
informative" and embodying "a positive approach." Both were restrained
and factual compared to the Bureau's anti-marijuana material of the
1930s. The Bureau's publication, "Living Death: The Truth about Drug
Addiction," prepared earlier "in deference to this demand [for informa-
tion] and for those who decide to go ahead with an educational program,"
was now quietly withdrawn.[11]

The Denver press carried its share of syndicated articles putting the
Bureau's case before the public. The stories rehearsed the Bureau's
plight—understaffed but accounting for more federal prisoners than any
other agency, and now faced with a new problem in youthful offenders
who often progressed from marijuana to heroin. "Marijuana," a Bureau

official said, "was sold mostly in small, dark 'dine and dance dives' where racial lines frequently meet or overlap."[12] The intimation of interracial sexual relations was not unintentional. The specter of white women made sexually available by drugs to non-white men had demonstrated its power as early as the 1870s and was effectively employed in Anslinger's own published works.

Anslinger outlined the Bureau's remedy for rising drug abuse to the Senate Crime Investigation Committee in June of 1950. Longer sentences, "a substantial increase in the authorized strength of the Bureau of Narcotics," witness protection, central files for criminal information, and more special city and state narcotic law enforcement squads would do the job. He stressed that the Bureau's appropriation had grown very little in twenty years and now supported twenty-five percent fewer agents. The commissioner reminded the senators that the Bureau, with "about two percent of the Federal criminal law enforcement personnel," accounted "for more than 10 percent of the persons committed to Federal penal institutions," including some of the country's biggest gangsters.[13]

In 1950 Congress failed to act on a bill introduced by Congressman Hale Boggs of Louisiana to increase drug penalties, and in 1951 the Bureau redoubled its efforts. The *Post* did its part, publishing a six-part series of syndicated articles on dope which acknowledged that the "opinions and conclusions expressed are largely those of federal narcotic authorities." The series stressed that organized crime used marijuana to recruit new narcotics customers. Anslinger's characterization of the Bureau as the "forgotten agency" underlined his plea for support of his plan.[14] On the strength of this second campaign, the Boggs bill was passed and signed into law on November 2, 1951.

The Boggs Act established a single schedule of stiff penalties for violations of all federal narcotic laws, providing for maximum fines of $2,000 and sentences of two to five years for first offenses, five to ten for second, and ten to twenty for third and subsequent offenses. Suspended sentences and probation were denied. The Bureau had lobbied hard for mandatory minimum sentences, arguing that time and again enforcement agencies' best efforts were undone by lenient judges. The Bureau's campaign for increased appropriations was as successful as its campaign for stiffer penalties. The Bureau's 1953 appropriation of $2,790,000 nearly doubled the 1949 amount of $1,450,000—a figure scarcely higher than the Bureau's original appropriation in 1930.[15]

Incredibly, within a few months of the Boggs Act's passage, the Bureau all but certified its success. "While it is still too early to appraise the effectiveness of this legislation," the Bureau cautioned, "an improvement in narcotic conditions has been noted and there were definite indications at the end of the year that the increase in teenage drug addiction has been halted." Increased seizures of narcotics the following year were attributed "in large measure to the Bureau's policy of directing its efforts toward large traffickers and sources of supply." This had been Bureau policy for twenty years. Large seizures prior to the Boggs Act had been interpreted as indicators that increasing traffic required expansion of the Bureau's force.[16]

Local Consequences of the Bureau's Campaign

In campaigning for the Boggs Act, the Bureau had encouraged the states to increase penalties and provide compulsory treatment. Compulsory treatment, however, required additional expenditures and proved particularly difficult to obtain. After several years of effort, the Bureau regretfully observed that the states "have not been particularly eager to adopt such legislation, perhaps because of the lack of proper facilities for treatment." Only New York had made even a partial beginning, although some states had jailed addicts as disorderly or committed them as inebriates or insane. In 1945 Colorado had acted in advance of most other states by allowing judges to commit habitual users to a state, county, or city hospital or institution or to a city or county jail until cured.[17]

Syndicated national features and wire service accounts of spectacular seizures and arrests elsewhere continued to dominate drug publicity in Colorado. Readers of "Rise in Teenage Dope Addiction Poses New Problem in Big Cities," an Associated Press story carried by the *Rocky Mountain News*, or of *Life*'s "Children in Peril" quite likely associated what they read with Denver, Pueblo, or Colorado Springs. Press attempts at gauging Colorado's drug problem almost invariably relied on accounts of federal enforcement obtained from the Bureau's Denver office. "Dope Case Arrests up 30–35% Here" and "Narcotic Sales Increase 33Pct. in Denver Region" captioned relatively prominent accounts of federal activities.

Federal enforcement dealt almost entirely with marijuana, but Agent Talent noted the ominous appearance of heroin.[18]

Agents were understandably reluctant to underestimate the serious-ness of the drug problem. Temperate reports made poor news and were likely to be hidden away in the papers. A Public Health Service doctor, for example, essentially agreed with Agent Talent on the local predominance of marijuana and the effectiveness of joint Bureau and Denver police ef-forts to deter heroin traffickers. But the doctor downplayed the issue: "Except for marijuana, there is simply no problem worth talking about in Denver." His remarks, accordingly, were buried far back in the *Post*. Not surprisingly, his story, "Heroin Addiction Here Discounted," received far less public attention than an article the competing *News* had carried three days earlier: "Addict, 14, Wants More Wild Crime and Sex." Nor is it surprising that a drug's menace should loom largest to the agency charged with its control. Sleeping pills, the Public Health Service doctor believed, accounted for most of Denver's heroin reports. But sleeping pills received no attention from the Bureau of Narcotics. When the federal Food and Drug Administration announced a campaign against improper drugstore sales of barbiturates in Denver, the Police Department, long accustomed to working with the Bureau, denied that abuse was extensive.[19]

The Bureau's concerted campaign for the Boggs Act had raised local public awareness of drug problems to the desired saturation point. The *Messenger* of the Colorado Women's Christian Temperance Union (WCTU) observed that a recent newspaper article had "brought to mind that there has been a great deal over the radio and in the papers about young people in schools smoking marijuana." Early in 1951 expressions of local con-cern, for which the narcotics publicists had labored hard, began to crys-tallize. A federal judge in Denver had earlier remarked on the "great social menace" of drugs and the increased local narcotics traffic before sentencing several of the fifty-four arrested "during a fall roundup of known users and peddlers of marijuana." The Colorado WCTU's 1951 annual convention pushed aside its preoccupation with alcohol, "the greatest of narcotics," long enough to pass a resolution citing "the sinister and sub-versive propaganda of narcotic purveyors" and to urge "local governing bodies" to vigilance and action.[20] Finally, and most difficult to achieve, private citizens were roused to express concern to their representatives and to ask what they might do. One Coloradan wrote to ask how "to stop the crime wave that is now sweeping the young adults of America," a crime wave impelled by drug use. The Bureau readily characterized such expressions as "an abundance of evidence that the general public wanted to strengthen not only the Federal law but also the State laws dealing with the narcotic traffic." The Bureau was prepared for such requests for "suggestions and model laws," replying that the concerned citizen could press for state penalties comparable to those in the Boggs Act.[21]

In early July of 1951, "two leading members of the Denver Junior Chamber of Commerce" met with Supervisor Talent, who stressed that drugs were a major source of crime. Representatives of the chamber, an organization "actively interested in a narcotics control crusade," then visited Governor Thornton to share their concern. Shortly thereafter, Thornton announced that studies at state institutions and his own experience on a parole board had convinced him "that many crimes in Colorado have stemmed from drug addiction as well as drink." Consequently, he had requested the first assistant attorney general to study the desirability of giving the existing law "more teeth," especially as it applied to drug buyers. Convinced of the problem's urgency, Thornton said he would consider including narcotic legislation in his call for action at the next legislative session.[22]

Colorado Stiffens Drug Penalties

When the special session of the legislature met in January of 1952, Senator Neal Bishop of Denver introduced a bill tripling existing penalties and providing the death penalty for sale of narcotics to minors. The senator's concern was evident. "I would much rather they would come out and shoot my child down with a machine gun," he said, "than to make a narcotics addict out of him." But his bill, Talent reported to Washington, was "considered too drastic," and the committee to which it was referred declined to print it. The Colorado State Crime Commission, however, with which Talent had worked "at great length," had produced its own bill. Talent was sure this bill would "meet the Bureau's approval."[23]

As originally printed, the commission's draft, introduced by Senator Stephen L. R. McNichols, provided the same schedule of penalties as the Boggs Act—a maximum fine of $2,000 for all offenses and terms of two to five years for a first offense, five to ten for a second, and ten to twenty for third and subsequent offenses. It further provided a term of ten to twenty years for sale to or enticement of a minor and banned suspended sentences and probation for all but first offenders.

When the House balked at the high penalties and the Senate refused amendment, the bill was sent to a conference committee from which it emerged strangely altered. Although the original bill had provided for a fine *and* a prison term, the new draft eliminated fines altogether and substituted a schedule of mandatory penitentiary sentences. Talent attributed the changes to his appearance before the committee. He had assured them that setting a fine of no more than $2,000 or a prison term made it possible "for a violation to be punished merely by the assessing of a nominal fine, as little as $5.00 or less." As finally passed on February 6, 1952, the act provided a term of one to ten years for first offenders, five to fifteen for second offenders. It retained the penalty of ten to twenty years for offenses involving minors, but dropped the prohibition of suspended sentence and probation. By the omission of the words *and subsequent*, however, the act failed to provide for penalties beyond the second offense. It was, Talent pointed out, "not as strong as we wanted" but "much stronger than the old penalty section," which had provided maximum penalties of $1,000 and five years.[24]

The bill's passage had been spurred by the announcement, the day after its introduction, of sixty-seven drug-related arrests throughout the region. When Governor Thornton signed the bill into law on February 19, he expressed his hope that the stiff sentences would deter any further growth of the drug problem and lead to its ultimate elimination in Colorado. Assurance came with extraordinary promptness. A little over a month after the act became effective, Supervisor Talent's assessment ran in the *Post* under the caption, "Stiffer Laws Cutting State Dope Traffic to All-time Low." The new penalties had driven a few big-time dealers out, Talent reported. He assured readers that "The chances of a Denver schoolboy or girl being given a stick of marijuana, while never great in the past, have been tremendously reduced." Because the state and federal laws now had "teeth in them," "we have noticed a great drop in cases during the past several months. In fact the traffic here is at an all-time low." Talent observed of federal drug cases, "Now I can't remember the last case we've had."[25]

His further remarks suggested an explanation of the sudden decline in federal arrests—the basis, at least in part, for his optimistic assessment. Since the passage of the Boggs Act the previous fall, he said, Bureau agents had been under orders to concentrate on bigger cases, leaving smaller ones to state and local officials who had been hard pressed to find dope peddlers and users. This candid admission clearly suggested that, although the Bureau had since 1930 claimed "big-time operators" for its own and left "small fry" to state and local authorities, Bureau agents prior to the passage of the Boggs Act had pursued small retail sellers and users. This course of enforcement would have produced first a sharp increase in federal arrests and then a sharp decline. The decline in federal arrests would be, at best, only partially made up when small-timers were again left to understaffed state and local officers.

Indicators of the Extent of Drug Use

Most knowledgeable national observers believed that drug users had increased in numbers significantly in the late 1940s and early 1950s, young drug users and marijuana users disproportionately so. Colorado enforcement statistics, Denver arrest records, and records of federal arrests in Colorado support these conclusions. Arrests for possession and sale of narcotics and marijuana in the federal district including Colorado, Utah, and Wyoming rose slowly but steadily between 1948 and 1952. Colorado enforcement activity rose from twenty-seven cases in 1945 to eighty-six in 1952—still short, however, of the record of eighty-seven arrests set in 1929 from a considerably smaller population. But the significance of this tripling of arrests is considerably altered if marijuana arrests are separated from "hard" drug violations. Of the 598 local arrests reported between 1945 and 1952, marijuana accounted for 395, or 66.1 percent. Neither had the distribution of violators by age changed significantly from the pre-war decade. Most striking was the increase in blacks arrested for drug violations, from less than one percent from 1933 to 1939 to 21.8 percent of comparable arrests between 1948 and 1952.[26]

There is, however, little evidence that evaluation of the extent and nature of Colorado's drug problems shaped the response of state legislators and city councilmen. The evidence is strong that local legislators and public officials deferred to the assessments and remedies of federal authorities, primarily the Bureau of Narcotics. Colorado's Act of 1952, for example, was born in considerable part of fears that drugs were being "pushed" to Colorado's schoolchildren. In the four years prior to the act, arrests in Denver of those under twenty years of age averaged four a year. By comparison, arrests for drunkenness attracted no attention but rose in Denver from 8,692 in 1945 to 19,559 in 1952, when drug arrests jumped to eighty-four.[27]

Colorado Marches in Step with the Bureau

The pattern of legislative response to Bureau initiative, fully evident in Colorado's Act of 1952, became even more pronounced in the late 1950s and early 1960s. This was particularly true of the Colorado legislature's acceptance of the heavy penalties the Bureau promoted. In July of 1956, Congress passed the Narcotic Control Act "to provide for a more effective control of narcotic drugs and marijuana." The act broadened the definition of marijuana-related criminal acts, but its major feature was an increase in penalties for violation of federal narcotic laws. The act set maximum fines of $20,000 for all offenses and prison terms ranging from five to twenty years for first-conviction trafficking and two to ten years for other first offenses, to ten to forty years for second and third convictions. It denied suspension and probation for all trafficking convictions and for all but first convictions for lesser offenses. Sales to juveniles were punishable by special penalties of ten to forty years and up to $20,000. The Narcotic Drug Import and Export Act was armed with special penalties for sale to juveniles of up to $20,000 in fines and sentences of ten years to life imprisonment or death.[28]

Consequently, George O. Weber, the Bureau's supervisor in Denver, was prepared when a Denver official called less than two months later to ask if Weber had suggestions for "any needed state narcotic legislation." Weber did indeed have a suggestion: The state could adopt the schedule of increased penalties recently provided by the Narcotic Control Act. After consulting with headquarters, Weber suggested that the definition of *narcotic drugs* be amended to include the formula, "any other drugs to which the federal laws relating to narcotic drugs may now apply, and any drug found by [state officers] . . . to have an addiction forming or addiction sustaining liability."[29]

Concerned civic organizations rallied behind the resulting bill, described by a spokeswoman for the Denver Women's Club as "imperative to prevent our youth from becoming addicts, potential killers and a menace to every community." As enacted on March 26, 1957, however, the measure more closely resembled the Colorado Act of 1952 than the federal Narcotic Control Act of 1956. The federal act's extreme penalties for sale to juveniles were rejected in favor of retaining the previous penalty of ten to twenty years. The earlier provision for commitment of addicts for an indefinite term had looked toward treatment, although it allowed simple imprisonment as well. Addicts were now simply defined as disorderly persons subject to terms of six months to one year in jail or the penitentiary. The omission of penalties for third and subsequent offenses was repeated, but the three new synthetics defined but not controlled in 1949 were at last restricted.[30]

The Narcotic Control Act of 1956 was the high point of the federal effort to control narcotic use with heavy penalties, but the crest was reached somewhat later in Colorado. In 1959 the legislature passed a narcotic drugs bill listing as sponsors no less than twenty-seven senators and eight representatives. The bill embodied minor regulatory changes and a penalty schedule of staggering complexity, exceeding in most respects the penalties provided in the federal Narcotic Control Act. Subsequent offenses were punishable by terms of as much as twenty, thirty, or forty years in prison. The Bureau's Denver supervisor had testified before the Senate committee in favor of the act's undeniable "teeth."[31]

In sharp contrast to the state's efforts to control illegal trafficking, regulation of the legitimate drug trade was knowledgeable and systematic. Several trade and professional organizations and their local affiliates continued to organize regulation of legitimate sales effectively, promoting carefully drafted legislation, frequently amended in response to developments within the trade. In 1953 alone the legislature passed four major bills revising the statutes governing the sale of hypnotics and poisons and the practice of pharmacy. By the end of 1955, public health authorities could report that fraud to obtain prescription narcotics was "at a very low level."[32]

The "Stiffer Penalties" Tide Crests

Colorado's reliance on heavy penalties reached its crest in 1963, when Governor John Love signed into law a bill providing death or life imprisonment for sale of narcotics to anyone under twenty. But by the early 1960s, the medical and legal professions were reacting adversely to the severity of the Bureau of Narcotics' punitive solution. Mental health professionals increasingly viewed addiction as a disease, rather than a crime. Drug use among middle-class children was growing. These developments and the demonstrable failures of past policy to control illicit use undercut the anti-drug consensus carefully orchestrated by the Bureau. Commissioner Anslinger's retirement in 1962 and the report of the White House Conference on Narcotics and Drug Abuse in 1963 favoring a "medical approach" marked the end of a century-long reliance on harsher penalties to curb drug use.[33]

In 1962, the U.S. Supreme Court found that addiction was a condition, not a crime, and ruled unconstitutional a law permitting the confinement of addicts, essentially similar to the provision adopted by Colorado in 1957 at the Bureau's suggestion. In 1964 a state judge in Boulder found that the legislature had improperly delegated to State Board of Health officials and federal authorities its responsibility for determining which drugs should be controlled. His decision invalidated most of the state's narcotic laws, which lacked a severability clause.

The conventional wisdom of narcotic regulation was not discarded overnight. The Bureau-trained head of the Denver Police Department's narcotics squad, citing the difficulty of enforcing existing laws, still looked for a solution in a mandatory ten-year minimum sentence. His reasoning reflected understandable discouragement with the failure of attempts to cure addicts. Without stiffer penalties, Colorado would be obliged to spend "millions of dollars for a medical facility to treat the user of narcotics," he warned, and with little likelihood of success. He displayed an unconscious cynicism in urging that harsher penalties would solve the problem for Colorado by causing users and dealers to "move their operations to another state with weaker laws."[34] In retrospect, it is clear that a century-long cycle in Colorado's response to "dope" was complete.

Conclusion

OLORADO'S attempt to control the use of habituating, addicting, and psychoactive drugs was ultimately unsuccessful. Drugs of abuse retained a relatively constant core in the opiates, cocaine, and marijuana. Criminalization of the illicit drug trade replaced "soft" drugs with "hard," no more difficult to smuggle and much more profitable. Few drugs of abuse disappeared, except to be replaced by more dangerous successors. A growing flood of newly synthesized drugs swept around the legal barriers erected to contain them. "Secondary" drugs—sedatives and hypnotics—attracted little attention, but may have accounted for the majority of illicit use.

As the responsibility for social problems moved from municipalities to the state legislature in the late 1890s and early 1900s, drug control moved with it. On the eve of World War I, progressive reformers committed the federal government to drug control with the Harrison Act. Thereafter, Colorado's meagerly supported state and local enforcement personnel shared jurisdiction with comparatively well supported and specialized federal narcotics agents. There could have been only one result. Colorado ceded first the lead and then the routine of enforcement, as federal agencies repeatedly pursued "small-time" users and dealers.

In popular view, illicit drug use cycled from personal vice and moral failing, to medical problem, to criminal act, to social pathology. New laws successfully reduced accidental medical addiction, thereby confining addiction to an even smaller element of the population. It then became easier to see drug use as the distinctive vice of others—an ethnic, racial, economic, or social minority. In the years following World War I, public sympathy was progressively withdrawn from the drug addict as addiction came to be associated first with "lower" races and "social defectives" and then with violence and crime. Consequently, when the nation acknowledged the failure of prohibition, only a few voices suggested that prohibition of drugs had failed as dismally.

Just when prohibition's failure might have opened an opportunity for reevaluation of drug policy, it was the nation's misfortune to obtain in Harry J. Anslinger an energetic and determined commissioner of the Bureau of Narcotics. Colorado's enactment of harsher narcotic laws in the early 1920s and early 1950s certainly coincided with heightened fear of outsiders and subversives. Colorado, however, increasingly responded not to local events but to tides of opinion directed by the Bureau.

Drug use in Colorado was a marginal public concern except when agitated to some particular end. The actual extent and patterns of usage, in fact, are scarcely better known to the public today than they were in 1914 when the Harrison Act was passed. Drug use was virtually invisible to the ordinary citizen. Public concern was effectively aroused only by accounts of sensational menace, regrettably often unsupported— or contradicted—by the available evidence.

Enforcement agencies could only imagine hitting the problem harder and harder. The record of nearly a hundred years suggests that stringent penalties not only failed to curb but may indeed have compounded the social costs of illicit drug use. A little over half a century after Colorado had enacted one of the earliest state laws against marijuana, it became one of the first states to provide for separate and milder penalties for its use. In the early 1960s, the United States stood on the threshold of an era of new drugs of abuse, new patterns of use, and new classes of users. Tentative signs suggested the possibility of a reevaluation of punitive controls, and Colorado appeared ready to reject ever more stringent penalties. That opportunity was lost in the social and political turmoil that engulfed the United States in the later 1960s and 1970s.

Notes

Chapter 1: Drugs of Habit in Nineteenth-Century Colorado

1

For an explanation of the effects of these drugs, their relationships, and brief histories, see Louis S. Goodman and Alfred Gilman, eds., *The Pharmacological Basis of Therapeutics*, 5th ed., rev. (New York: Macmillan, 1975), ch. 2, "History and Theories of General Anaesthesia"; ch. 10, "Hypnotics and Sedatives, Miscellaneous Agents"; ch. 15, "Narcotic Analgesics and Antagonists."

2

Colorado, Board of Health, *Annual Report*, 1879, 11.

3

Colorado Miner (Georgetown), 28 April 1870, 26 May 1870.

4

John Smith, *The Mysteries of Opium Revealed* (London, 1700), cited in David F. Musto, *The American Disease: Origins of Narcotic Control* (New Haven and London: Yale University Press, 1973), 69; H. von Ziemssen, ed. (American ed. Albert H. Buck), *A Cyclopaedia of the Practice of Medicine* (New York: W. Wood and Co., 1878), 18:856–75; E. Harris Ruddock, *Test Book of Modern Medicine and Surgery on Homeopathic Principles* (London: Homeopathic Publishing Co., 1881), 928–29; Albert H. Buck, ed., *A Reference Book of the Medical Sciences* (New York: W. Wood and Co., 1887), 5:326–33.

5

Ray V. Pierce, *The People's Common Sense Medical Adviser* (Buffalo: World's Dispensary Printing, 1879), 829–31; J. H. Pulte, *The Homeopathic Domestic Physician*, 13th ed. (Cincinnati: Smith and Worthington, 1879), 79.

6

Fairplay Flume, 7 July 1879; Richard Quain, ed., *A Dictionary of Medicine* (New York: D. Appleton and Co., 1883), 1,068; *A Cyclopaedia of the Practice of Medicine* 17:844; Territory of Colorado, *Session Laws*, 1872, 157–59; Denver, *Charter and Ordinances*, 1875, ch. 6, art. 2, sec. 2, 78; Denver, *Charter and Ordinances*, 1884, ch. 7, art. 2, secs. 37, 38, 182–83.

7

Weekly Central City Register, 14 January 1874; *Rocky Mountain News*, 14 September 1873, 17 October 1875.

8

Charles E. Terry and Mildred Pellens, *The Opium Problem* (New York: Committee on Drug Addictions in collaboration with the Bureau of Social Hygiene, 1928), 73, 807–8; *Leadville Chronicle*, 16 June 1879; *Rocky Mountain News*, 30 October 1879.

9

Denver Tribune, 12 October 1880; *Rocky Mountain News*, 9 October 1880, 12 October 1880.

10

Rocky Mountain News, 12 October 1880, 13 October 1880.

11
Denver Tribune, 12 October 1880; *Rocky Mountain News*, 31 October 1880, 1 November 1880, 2 November 1880; *Denver Daily Times*, 1 November 1880; and generally, Roy T. Wortman, "Denver's Anti-Chinese Riot, 1880," *The Colorado Magazine* 42(fall 1965):275–91, *Denver Post*, 27 October 1996.

12
Denver, *Charter and Ordinances*, 1881, Ord. 15, ch. 6, art. 4, 113–14; *Denver Daily Times*, 30 December 1880; *Rocky Mountain News*, 30 December 1880, 31 December 1880.

13
Rocky Mountain News, 12 December 1880, 6 January 1881, 29 March 1881, 20 July 1881, 10 May 1884, 10 January 1885.

14
Alonzo Calkins, *Opium and the Opium Habit* (Philadelphia: J. B. Lippincott and Co., 1871); S. F. McFarlin, *Opium Inebriety and the Hypodermic Syringe*, Transactions of the New York State Medical Society, 1877; C. Allbutt, "On the Abuse of the Hypodermic Injections of Morphia," *The Practitioner* 5(1870):327; H. H. Kane, *The Hypodermic Injection of Morphine* (New York: C. L. Bermingham and Co., 1880), cited in Terry and Pellens, *The Opium Problem*, 69–73.

15
George Miller Beard, *American Nervousness: Its Causes and Consequences* (New York: G. P. Putnam's Sons, 1881); "Quackery and the Quacked," *National Quarterly Review* 2(1861): 354, cited in Musto, *American Disease*, 276; O. Marshall, "The Opium Habit in Michigan in 1877," *Sixth Annual Report of the State Board of Health for the Fiscal Year Ended September 30, 1878* (Lansing, Mich.: State Board of Health, 1878).

16
"Morphinism," *Denver Medical Times* 22(1903):392.

17
Frank P. Foster, ed., *Reference Book of Practical Therapeutics*, 3d ed. (New York: D. Appleton and Co., 1897), 1:iv.

18
Pueblo Chieftain, 31 October 1880, advertisement for "Tolu Rock and Rye."

19
Rocky Mountain News, 16 March 1885.

20
Poster in author's collection.

21
"Morphinism," *Denver Medical Times* 22(1903):391; *Rocky Mountain News*, 30 March 1880.

22
Pierce, *Common Sense Medical Adviser*, 385; Foster, *Practical Therapeutics* 2:223, 1:34.

23
Rocky Mountain News, 10 January 1885.

24
U.S. Department of the Treasury, Public Health Service, *State Laws Relating to the Control of Narcotic Drugs and the Treatment of Drug Addiction*, supplement to *Public Health Reports* 91(Washington, D.C.: Government Printing Office, 1931):2; Colorado Women's Christian Temperance Uni-

on (WCTU), *Messenger*, February 1930; Colorado, *Laws Passed at the Sixth Session of the General Assembly of the State of Colorado*, 1887, 378–79; Colorado, *Senate Journal of the General Assembly of the State of Colorado*, 6th sess., 1887, entries for SB 173, SB 133; Colorado, *House Journal of the General Assembly of the State of Colorado*, 6th sess., 1887, entries for HB 82.

25
Denver, *Charter and Ordinances*, 1898, Ord. 101, ch. 8, art. 7, sec. 606, 344–46.

26
J. C. Mulhall, *New York Medical Journal*, 30 November 1895, cited in Foster, *Practical Therapeutics* 2:307; *New York Times*, 1885, cited in Maurine B. Neuberger, *Smoke Screen: Tobacco and the Public Welfare* (Englewood Cliffs, N.J.: Prentice-Hall, 1963), 52; Jerome E. Brooks, *The Mighty Leaf: Tobacco through the Centuries* (Boston: Little, Brown, 1952), 253.

27
Pueblo Chieftain, 13 November 1880, advertisement for "D.I.C." cure.

28
Advertisement in *American Medical Journal*, 1873, cited in Robert A. Buerki, "Medical Views on Narcotics and Their Effects in the Mid-1890s," *Pharmacy in History* 17(January 1975):37.

29
Foster, *Practical Therapeutics* 2:46; *Rocky Mountain News*, 12 December 1880; Foster, *Practical Therapeutics* 1:451; *Rocky Mountain News*, 4 April 1887.

30
Denver Medical Times 6(August1887): 342, 4(February 1885):243–44, 25(October 1905):216; Carl Ubbelohde, Maxine Benson, and Duane A. Smith, *A Colorado History*, 3d ed. (Boulder, Colo.: Pruett Publishing Co., 1972), 149.

31
Rocky Mountain News, 28 October 1892; *Denver City Directory*, 1891–1921, entries under "Gold Cure Treatment"; *Denver Medical Times* 21(July 1901):11; 25(October 1905):216; *Denver Post*, 13 February 1895; *Denver City Directory*, 1891–1921 (esp. 1893, 1,253).

32
Colorado Medicine 1(December 1904): 369.

33
Horatio C. Wood and Reginald H. Fitz, *The Practice of Medicine* (Philadelphia: J. B. Lippincott, 1897), 368; *Denver Medical Times* 23(January 1903):3.

34
Colorado, *Session Laws*, 1893, ch. 100, 283–85.

35
Foster, *Practical Therapeutics* 1:454; Colorado, *Biennial Report of the Colorado Insane Asylum*, 1903–1904, 10.

36
Colorado, *Session Laws*, 1895, ch. 74, 172–75; 1911, ch. 146, 447–50.

37
Ibid., 1897, ch. 38, 138.

38
Denver, Ord. 75, published in *Denver*

Republican, 22 July 1898, in *Denver City Ordinances* (April 1891–December 1927), scrapbooks compiled by F. A. Williams, vol. 8, series 1898, 95, Government Publications and Business Division, Denver Public Library (DPL); *Denver Times*, 7 July 1898.

39
Rocky Mountain News, 10 October 1886; Denver, *Charter and Ordinances*, 1886, ch. 7, art. 1, secs. 11, 28, 348–49, 387.

40
Denver Times, 1 February 1899, 18 May 1899, 17 July 1901, 1 October 1901.

41
Colorado, Board of Health, *Sixth Report*, 1900–1902, "Report of A. L. Bennett, Medical Inspector to Chinese," 206; *Seventh Report*, 1902–1904, "Report of A. L. Bennett, Medical Inspector to Chinese," 62.

42
Ibid., *Fourth Report*, 1892–93, 188–92.

43
Denver Times, 11 May 1902; *Denver Post*, 22 October 1905.

44
J. H. Beal, "An Anti-Narcotic Law," *Proceedings of the American Pharmaceutical Association* 51(1903):478, and "Draft of an Anti-Narcotic Law," 486.

45
Compiled from Colorado, Department of Health, *Biennial Report of Colorado Insane Asylum*, 1887–88, 1889–90, 1891–92, 1893–94, 1895–96, 1897–98, 1899–1900, "Tables of Supposed Cause of Insanity."

46
John Elsner, "Reminiscences at Annual Dinner of the Staff of the National Jewish Hospital for Consumptives," *Denver Medical Times* 28(July 1908):7.

47
Colorado, Board of Health, *Fourth Report*, 1892–93, 188–89; "Cyphilene: A Magic Cure," *Denver Times*, 16 June 1901; regarding the Ludan Medical Institute for "nervous, sexual, and private diseases," see *Denver Times*, 18 August 1901.

48
J. E. Courtney, "Report of Cases of Morphinism," *Colorado Medicine* 3(January 1906):19–27; J. N. Hall, "Significance of Epigastric Pain and Tenderness," *Colorado Medicine* 1 (March 1904):177; Edwin K. Knowles, "Narcotic Addiction and Its Treatment," *Colorado Medicine* 8(August 1911):290.

Chapter 2: The Reformers Turn to State Regulation

1
Denver Post, 22 October 1905, sec. 3.

2
Denver Times, 29 January 1903, 13 April 1903, 14 April 1903.

3
Ibid., 10 May 1902, 11 May 1902, 12 May 1902.

4
James H. Beal, "Report of the Committee on the Acquirement of the Drug Habit," *Proceedings of the American Pharmaceutical Association* 51 (1903):466–76.

5
"Draft of An Anti-Narcotic Law," *Proceedings of the American Pharmaceutical Association* 51(1903):486. Denver, *Code*, 1906, Ord. 101, ch. 18, secs. 786–92; *Denver Post*, 18 November 1914, sec. 2.

6
George E. Pettey, "Narcotic Drug Addictions: Pathology, Treatment, Prognosis," *Colorado Medicine* 1(December 1904):424.

7
Colorado, *Session Laws*, 1907, ch. 224, 582–83.

8
U.S. Department of the Treasury, Public Health Service, "A Digest of the Laws and Regulations in Force in the United States Relating to Possession, Use, Sale and Manufacture of Poisons and Habit-Forming Drugs," by Martin I. Wilbert, *Public Health Bulletin* 6(November 1912):43. Colorado, Department of Health, *Ninth Biennial Report*, 1907–1908, 12.

9
Denver Post, 22 October 1905, sec. 3. *Denver Sunday News-Times*, 5 September 1909. "Narcotics," Western History Clippings File (WHCF), DPL.

10
Rocky Mountain News, 24 March 1946; *Denver Post*, 31 July 1908.

11
Assistant Secretary of State Robert Bacon to Harvey W. Wiley, Head, Bureau of Chemistry, U.S. Department of Agriculture, 4 November 1908, Records of the Bureau of Chemistry, Department of Agriculture, RG 97, File 140, National Archives and Records Administration (NARA), Washington, D.C., cited in Musto, *American Disease*, 34. *Denver Post*, 17 July 1909, sec. 1; *Denver Republican*, 22 July 1911 (WHCF).

12
Elliott West, "Of Lager Beer and Sonorous Songs," *The Colorado Magazine* 48(1971):118, 128; *Denver Post*, 2 February 1909. Wilbert, "Digest of the Laws," 5.

13
U.S. Congress, House Committee on Ways and Means, *The Importation and Use of Opium: Hearings before the Committee of Ways and Means*, 61st Cong., 3d sess., 1910, 32.

14
U.S. Congress, Senate, 61st Cong., 3d sess., 1912, S. Doc. 736, 57.

15
Knowles, "Narcotic Addiction," 286–87.

16
E. G. Eberle, "Narcotics and Habitués," *Proceedings of the American Pharmaceutical Association* 50(1902):636-37. Beal, "An Anti-Narcotic Law," 479. *Denver Post*, 22 October 1905, sec. 3.

17
Colorado, *Session Laws*, 1911, ch. 96, 245–47.

18
U.S. Department of the Treasury, Public Health Service, "The Number and Kind of Drug Addicts," by Martin I. Wilbert, Reprint No. 294 from *Public Health Service Reports* (August 1915), 1. Knowles, "Narcotic Addiction," 287.

19
U.S. Department of the Treasury, Office of the Commissioner of Internal Revenue, "Traffic in Narcotic Drugs: Report of the Special Committee of Investigation Appointed March 25, 1918, by the Secretary of the Treasury" (June 1919), 258.

20
F. A. Williams, comp., *Denver City Ordinances* 27, Ord. 20, series 1912, 91, 92; Ord. 45, series 1912, 188–89 (DPL).

21
Rocky Mountain News, 22 January 1913.

22
Alexander Lambert, "The Obliteration of the Craving for Narcotics," *Journal of the American Medical Association* 53(September 1909):985–89; Knowles, "Narcotic Addiction," 287.

23
Denver Post, 23 August 1949, 18 November 1914.

24
Rocky Mountain News, 15 August 1914; *Denver Post*, 18 November 1914, sec. 2.

25
Denver Post, 11 March 1914.

26
Denver Post, 18 November 1914, sec. 2.

27
Ibid.

28
Musto, *American Disease*, ch. 2, esp. 39.

29
U.S. Congress, Senate, 61st Cong., 3d sess., 1912, S. Doc. 736, 58, 59. Hamilton Wright to Joseph Remington, 26 April 1910, Papers of Dr. Hamilton Wright, RG 43, entry 51, NARA.

30
Note on the Harrison Bill, *Journal of the American Pharmaceutical Association* 2(February 1913):138. James H. Beal, "The Federal Anti-Narcotic Situation," *Journal of the American Pharmaceutical Association* 2(July 1913): 821.

31
"Report of the Committee to Cooperate with the State Pharmacal Association," *Colorado Medicine* 11(October 1914):387–88.

32
"Report of the Committee to Cooperate with the State Pharmacal Association," *Colorado Medicine* 12(November 1915):341. Colorado, State Board of Pharmacy, "Thirty-fifth Annual Report of the State Board of Pharmacy of Colorado for the Year Ending July 2, 1928," 110–14; "Rules and Regulations for the Enforcement of the Colorado Narcotic Drugs Act Adopted by the Colorado State Board of Health, July 8, 1915."

33
Denver Post, 13 January 1915.

34
"Report of the Committee to Cooperate with the State Pharmacal Association," *Colorado Medicine* 11(February 1914):31.

35
Wilbert, "Number and Kind of Drug Addicts," 1.

36
U.S. Department of the Treasury, Public Health Service, "A Digest of the Laws and Regulations in Force in the United States Relating to Possession, Use, Sale and Manufacture of Poisons and Habit-Forming Drugs, Supplement No. 2," by Martin I. Wilbert. Reprint No. 240 from *Public Health Service Reports* (1915), 14. *Denver Post*, 1 August 1915, sec. 1.

37
Denver Times, 29 April 1915; *Rocky Mountain News*, 30 April 1915. *Denver Post*, 19 July 1919.

38
Denver Post, 12 January 1917; Colorado, *Session Laws*, 1917, ch. 2, 7; Omer C. Stewart, "Peyote and Colorado's Inquisition Law," *Colorado Quarterly* 5(summer 1956):79.

39
Denver Times, 29 October 1899, sec. 3; *Denver Post*, 4 June 1917; Stewart, "Peyote," 79.

40
Colorado, *Session Laws*, 1917, ch. 39, 120; U.S. Department of Commerce, Bureau of the Census, *Thirteenth Census of the United States, 1910: Population*, 2:905, 922, 929. *Fourteenth Census of the United States, 1920: Population*, 2:31; Richard J. Bonnie and Charles H. Whitebread, *The Marihuana Conviction: A History of Marihuana Prohibition in the United States* (Charlottesville: University Press of Virginia, 1974), 37.

41
U.S. Department of the Treasury, Bureau of Internal Revenue, *Annual Report of the Commissioner of Internal Revenue for the Fiscal Year Ended 30 June 1915*, 29.

42
Robert P. Walton, *Marijuana: America's New Drug Problem* (Philadelphia, 1938); Bonnie and Whitebread, *Marihuana Conviction*, 151.

43
Ibid., 24.

44
W. G. Campbell, Acting Chief, Bureau of Chemistry, to B. C. Keith, Bureau of Internal Revenue, 22 April 1918, Records of the Bureau of Internal Revenue, RG 170, File 0810, NARA.

45
Colorado, *Session Laws*, 1919, ch. 116, 399.

Chapter 3: The Expanding Federal Role

1
"Harrison Narcotic Act Effective," *Colorado Medicine* 12(February 1915): 37; U.S. Department of the Treasury, Public Health Service, "The Harrison Anti-Narcotic Law: The Effect of Its Enforcement on the Drug Addicts," by Murray G. Motter, *Public Health Service Reports* (April 1915), reprinted in *Colorado Medicine* 12(February 1915): 160–61.

2
"Traffic in Narcotic Drugs," 24, 16, 10, 14. *Denver Times*, 28 June 1919.

3
"Traffic in Narcotic Drugs," 10, 14.

4
Wilbert, "Digest of the Laws," 2.

5
Musto, *American Disease*, 125–28; regarding Treasury Decision 2112 implementing the Harrison Act, see *Annual Report of the Commissioner of Internal Revenue*, 1915, 169.

6
U.S. v. Jin Fuey Moy, 241 U.S. 394, 5 June 1916; Rufus G. King, "The Narcotic Bureau and the Harrison Act: Jailing the Healers and the Sick," *Yale Law Journal* 62(April 1953):736–49.

7
U.S. v. Doremus, 246 Fed. Rep. 958, March 1919; *Webb et al. v. U.S.*, 249 U.S. 96, 1919; *Jin Fuey Moy v. U.S.*, 254 U.S. 189, 1920. *U.S. v. Behrman*, 258 U.S. 280, 1921; Musto, *American Disease*, ch. 6, esp. 130–36; *Lindner v. U.S.*, 268 U.S. 5, 18, 1925, at 15 and 20; King, "Jailing the Healers," 739; King, "Note on Narcotics Regulation," *Yale Law Journal* 62(April 1953):744–45.

8
A. G. Dingley, "Workings and Improvements of the Harrison Anti-Narcotic Law," *Colorado Medicine* 17 (January 1920):1–6.

9
Ibid., 5; "Discussion" of Agent Dingley's Report, *Colorado Medicine* 17 (January 1920):6–9.

10
Colorado, Board of Health, "Report of the State Detention Home of Women with Venereal Disease," *Twelfth Report*, 1921–22, 20; *Thirteenth Report*, 1923–24, 16; Colorado, Board of Health, *Report of the Insane Asylum*, 1891–92, 17; 1911–12, 25; *Report of the State Hospital*, 1921–22.

11
Colorado, Board of Health, *Report of the State Hospital*, 1921–22, 17, 18. H. A. LaMoure to State Board of Health, 30 November 1923, in Colorado, Board of Health, *Thirteenth Report*, 1923, 41. *Fourteenth Report*, 1924, 9.

12
"Report of the Supervisor of the Reformatory," Colorado, Board of Health, *Seventeenth Report*, 1928, 66. "Change the Prison to a Hospital," *Colorado Medicine* 20(September 1923):230–32; Lawrence Kolb, "Types and Characteristics of Drug Addicts," *Mental Hygiene* 9(1925):301; Kolb, "Drug Addiction in Its Relation to Crime," *Mental Hygiene* 9(1925):77; George S. Johnson, "The Uses of Narcosan in the Treatment of Drug Addiction," *Colorado Medicine* 24(November 1927): 347–49.

13
Denver Post, 23 June 1922.

14
Ibid., 28 November 1921.

15
J. McFadzean, "The Mexican from the Viewpoint of the Medical Practitioner," *Colorado Medicine* 3(May 1906): 133–35; U.S. Department of Commerce, Bureau of the Census, *Thirteenth Census of the United States, 1910: Population*, 2:905, 922, 929; *Fourteenth Census of the United States, 1920: Population*, 2:31; Colorado, Immigration Bureau, *Yearbook of the State of Colorado, 1928–29*, 266.

16
Denver Times, 27 April 1922; Colorado WCTU, *Messenger*, February 1921;

Women's Club of Denver, *Annual Announcement* 21–31 (1915–25).

17
F. A. Williams, comp., *Denver City Ordinances* 42, Ord. 37, series 1922, 4 (DPL).

18
Colorado, Immigration Bureau, *Yearbook of the State of Colorado, 1927–28,* 239.

19
U.S. Department of the Treasury, Bureau of Internal Revenue, *Annual Report of the Commissioner of Internal Revenue, Extracts*, 1922, 3; *Denver Post*, 30 December 1923, sec. 2.

20
Denver Post, 30 December 1925.

21
All figures related to enforcement of the Harrison Act compiled from *Annual Report of the Commissioner of Internal Revenue*, 1915–22, *Annual Report of the Commissioner of Prohibition*, 1923–30, *Annual Report of the Commissioner of Narcotics*, 1931–34.

22
Denver Post, 8 February 1927; Julia Bruns, "My Thrills and Horrors as a Drug Slave," *Post*, 28 November 1926–13 February 1927 (magazine).

23
U.S. Department of Commerce, Bureau of the Census, *Fifteenth Census of the United States, 1930: Population*, Mexicans in Pueblo; Colorado, *Session Laws*, 1927, ch. 95, 309–11.

24
Colorado, *House Journal of the General Assembly of the State of Colorado,* *27th Session*, 1927, entries for HB 477.

25
Denver Post, 21 February 1927, 24 September 1928.

26
Ibid., 30 December 1928 (magazine). *Rocky Mountain News*, 27 March 1929.

27
Denver Post, 10 January 1929; Colorado, *Session Laws*, 1929, ch. 93, 331; Colorado, *Senate Journal of the General Assembly of the State of Colorado, 28th Session*, 1929, entries for SB 409.

28
Richard C. Callen to Lawrence C. Phipps, late 1926 or early 1927, Records of the Bureau of Narcotics, RG 170, File 0480–36, NARA.

29
Levi G. Nutt to Lawrence C. Phipps, 25 January 1929; Phipps to Nutt, 26 January 1929; Phipps to Nutt, 6 January 1929; Phipps to Nutt, 8 April 1929, Records of the Bureau of Narcotics, RG 170, File 0480–36, NARA.

Chapter 4: Marijuana and the Bureau of Narcotics

1
U.S. Congress, Senate, *A Bill to Amend the Act of May 26, 1922, the Narcotic Drugs Import and Export Act*, SB 2075, 71st Cong., 1st sess., 1929; Secretary of the Treasury Andrew W. Mellon to W. T. Carruth, Chairman, Committee on Finance, 16 December 1929; Mellon to Reed Smoot, 21 December 1929, File 0480–36, NARA.

2
Nutt to Phipps, 4 January 1930, Records of the Bureau of Narcotics, RG 170, File 0480–36, NARA. *Denver Post*, 2 February 1930.

3
Nutt to Phipps, 4 January 1930, File 0480–36; U.S. Congress, House, *A Bill to Establish Narcotic Farms*, HB 13645, 71st Cong., 1st sess., 1929, Pub. L. 672, 19 January 1929; *Denver Post*, 30 March 1929, 16 October 1929, 2 February 1930.

4
Harry Anslinger and Will Oursler, *The Murderers: The Story of the Narcotic Gangs* (New York: Farrar, Straus, and Cudahy, 1961), 20.

5
U.S. Congress, House Committee ("Wickersham Commission"), *Enforcement of the Prohibition Laws of the United States*, H. Doc. 722, 71st Cong., 3d sess., 1931, 1–84 (summary); cited in James E. Hansen, "Moonshine and Murder: Prohibition in Denver," *The Colorado Magazine* 50(L/1, 1973): 17; Philip Van Cise to Governor William E. Sweet, 29 December 1923, Records of the Office of the Governor, William E. Sweet, 1923–25, Correspondence, 1923, Box 6; R. C. Valentine, Chief of Legal Section, Bureau of Prohibition, to Nutt, 27 September 1923; Valentine, "Memorandum for Colonel Nutt," 8 October 1923, File 0810, NARA.

6
National Conference of Commissioners on Uniform State Laws, *Handbook of the National Commissioners on Uniform State Laws*, 1928, 76–77.

7
U.S. Department of the Treasury, *Annual Report of the Commissioner of Internal Revenue, Excerpts*, 1927, 3. Conference of State and Provincial Health Authorities, *Report of the Commission on Drugs to the Conference of State and Provincial Health Authorities*, 1926, 9.

8
Arthur Woods, *Dangerous Drugs: The World Fight against Illicit Drug Traffic in Narcotics* (New Haven, 1931), 62; Charles J. Clayton, Secretary, Colorado Pharmacal Association, to Phipps, 20 March 1930, File 0145, No. 1, NARA.

9
U.S. Department of the Treasury, Bureau of Narcotics, *Traffic in Opium and Other Dangerous Drugs for the Year Ended December 31, 1930*, 11, 12.

10
U.S. Department of the Treasury, Bureau of Narcotics, *Annual Report of the Commissioner of Narcotics for the Fiscal Year Ended December 31, 1931*, 23; *Traffic in Opium*, 1931, 14–16.

11
Annual Report of the Commissioner of Narcotics, 1931, 23. *Traffic in Opium*, 1930, 12.

12
U.S. Department of the Treasury, Bureau of Prohibition, *Annual Report of the Commissioner of Prohibition, Extracts in Regard to the Enforcement of the Narcotic Laws*, 1929, 11, 13; 1930, 11, 13; *Annual Report of the Commissioner of Narcotics*, 1931, Table 7, 44.

13
Colorado WCTU, *Messenger*, February 1930.

14
L. P. McQuillin to Harry J. Anslinger, 11 June 1931, File 0480–36, NARA.

15
Christian Science Monitor, 12 September 1931; Paul L. Warnshuis, "Crime and Criminal Justice among the Mexicans of Colorado," *Enforcement of the Prohibition Laws of the United States* 10, 265–329.

16
Christian Science Monitor, 3 October 1931.

17
Rocky Mountain News, 27 September 1931, 27 December 1931.

18
Annual Report of the Commissioner of Prohibition, 1930, 13; *Annual Report of the Commissioner of Narcotics*, 1931, 44; Colorado, State Planning Commission, *Yearbook of the State of Colorado, 1937–38*, "Narcotic Law Operations," 395; Denver, Department of Public Safety, Police Department, *Annual Report to the Denver Police Department*, 1930, 21; 1931, 21; 1932, 18; 1933, 48–49; 1934, 48–50; 1935, 69–70.

19
"Violators of the City Narcotic Law Confined to the Denver County Jail, July 1st, 1931, to January 30th, 1933," forwarded by H. S. Forrer to Anslinger, 27 February 1933, File 0480, No. 1, NARA.

20
Colorado, Colorado Psychopathic Hos-

pital, "Toxic Psychoses (Exogenous Group Drugs)," University of Colorado School of Medicine *Bulletin* 3 (August 1930), Table 1.

21
Denver Post, 8 December 1934, 9 December 1934. Anslinger to Col. Sharman, Department of Pensions and National Health, Canada, 27 December 1934, File 0480–36, NARA.

22
J. A. Manning to Anslinger, 16 August 1934, File 0480–36, NARA; *Denver Post*, 24 November 1933, 15 August 1934; *Rocky Mountain News*, 3 August 1934.

23
Assistant Secretary of the Treasury Stephen B. Gibbons to Secretary of State Cordell Hull, 3 October 1934, File 0480–36, NARA.

24
Anslinger to Senator Bronson Cutting, New Mexico, draft, sent over signature of General Counsel Oliphant, 17 March 1934, File 0480–36, NARA.

25
Louis Ruppel, Acting Commissioner, to Manning, 24 July 1934; Manning to the Commissioner of Narcotics, 1 August 1934, File 0480–36, NARA.

26
Ordinance "suggested for enactment in communities in those States which have not adopted the Uniform Narcotic Drug Act," File 0480–36, NARA.

27
Gibbons to Secretary of Agriculture Henry A. Wallace, attention L. H. Dewey, Bureau of Plant Industry, 14 April 1934; Gibbons to Hull, 3 Octo-

ber 1934, File 0480–36, NARA.

28
Memorandum, n.d. (early 1932), File
Uniform Narcotic Drug Act, 1, NARA.

29
Ibid., 3.

30
Traffic in Opium, 1935, v; Anslinger
to Dr. William C. Woodward, March
1935, draft, subsequently rewritten,
cited in Bonnie and Whitebread,
Marihuana Conviction, 95–97; *Traffic
in Opium*, 1938, 1.

31
Anslinger to Governor of Colorado, 10
January 1933, File 1960–9, NARA.

32
Courtney Ryley Cooper, *Here's to
Crime*, cited in Frederick T. Merrill,
Marihuana: The New Dangerous Drug
(Washington, D.C., 1938), 31; *Florida
Times-Union* (Jacksonville), 19 Octo-
ber 1933; Isabelle A. O'Neill to Colo-
rado Secretary of State, 6 January
1934, File 1960–9, NARA; *Denver
Post*, 15 November 1934.

33
Rocky Mountain News, 11 December
1934 (editorial), 20 December 1934;
Denver Post, 11 December 1934, 6
August 1937; interview with Roy L.
Cleere, M.D., Denver, April 1976.

34
Anslinger to Monte L. Powell, 1 October 1934; Powell to Anslinger, 31 October 1934, File 1960–9, NARA; Walter L. Treadway to West, 25 July
1932, cited in Bonnie and Whitebread,
Marihuana Conviction, 87; Manning

to Anslinger, 24 October 1934, File
1960–9, NARA.

35
Edwin C. Johnson to Anslinger, 9
January 1935; Anslinger to Man-
ning, 12 February 1935, File 1960–9,
NARA.

36
Rocky Mountain News, 4 February
1935 (editorial).

37
John D. Cunningham to Bureau of
Narcotics, 13 February 1938, File
1960–9, NARA.

38
Manning to T. E. Childers, 11 Febru-
ary 1935; Manning to Anslinger
("Confidential"), 12 February 1935;
Manning to Anslinger, 21 February
1935, File 1960–9, NARA.

39
Manning to Will S. Wood, Acting Com-
missioner, Bureau of Narcotics, 1
March 1935; Manning to Clifton
Mathews, U.S. District Attorney, Phoe-
nix, 26 February 1935; Mathews to
Manning, 4 March 1935, File 1960–
9, NARA.

40
Colorado, *Session Laws*, 1935, ch. 107,
370–91; *House Journal*, 31st sess.,
1935, entries for HB 138; *Senate Journal*, 31st sess., 1935, entries for HB
138. Colorado, *Session Laws*, 1935,
ch. 106, 366–69; *House Journal*, 31st
sess., 1935, entries for HB 557; *Senate Journal*, 31st sess., 1935, entries
for HB 557. Manning to Anslinger, 27
March 1935; Manning to Anslinger,
28 March 1935, File 1960–9, NARA.

41
Will S. Wood to Edwin C. Johnson, 9
April 1935; Johnson to Wood, 19 April
1935, File 1960–9, NARA.

42
Manning to Wood, 3 May 1935; Wood
to Manning, 8 May 1935, File 1960–
9, NARA.

43
M. F. Haralson to Anslinger, 5 Febru-
ary 1936; Anslinger to Haralson, 12
February 1936, File 1960–9, NARA.

*Chapter 5: Colorado and the
Marijuana Tax Act*

1
Secretary of the Treasury to Sam
Rayburn, Chairman, House Committee on Interstate and Foreign Commerce, 13 March 1935, draft, File
0480–36, NARA; *Traffic in Opium*,
1937, 17, 54. U.S. Congress, House
Committee on Appropriations, *Hearings on Treasury Department Appropriations Bill for 1936*, H.R., 74th
Cong., 1st sess., 1935, 210.

2
Interstate Commission on Crime, "Re-
cent Extension of Federal Criminal
Law," Gordon Dean, Special Assistant
Attorney General, *Handbook*, 1938,
111.

3
U.S. Congress, House Committee on
Appropriations, *Hearings on Treasury
Department Appropriations Bill for
1936*, H.R., 74th Cong., 1st sess.,
1935, 211; *Traffic in Opium*, 1935, v.

4
Traffic in Opium, 1936, 74; 1937, 9,
10.

5
Colorado, Board of Health, *Annual Re-
port*, 1937, 19–20. U.S. Congress,
House, *Hearings before the House
Committee on Ways and Means on
H.R. 6385*, 75th Cong., 1st sess., 1937,
26.

6
Arthur C. Millspaugh, *Crime Control
by the National Government*, The Institute for Government Research of
the Brookings Institution, *Studies in
Administration* 34(Washington, D.C.:
The Brookings Institution, 1937):296,
vii.

7
Traffic in Opium, 1935, 3; 1937, 4;
1938, 50. Also 1935, iv.

8
Ibid., 1935, iv; 1937, 19.

9
Harry Anslinger and J. Gregory, *The
Protectors: The Heroic Story of the
Narcotics Agents, Citizens, and Offi-
cials in Their Unending, Unsung
Battles against Organized Crime in
America* (New York: Farrar, Straus,
1964), 20–21; Anslinger and Oursler,
Murderers, 20; Merrill, *Marihuana*,
27–28; Earl Albert Rowell and Robert
Rowell, *On the Trail of Marihuana—
the Weed of Madness* (Mountain View,
Calif., 1939), 69–74; both Merrill and
Earl Albert Rowell suggested that the
Marijuana Tax Act might increase
the profit in trafficking in marijuana sufficiently to attract organized
crime—Rowell bluntly and repeatedly enough that it likely contributed
to his fall from favor with the Bureau
of Narcotics.

10
Traffic in Opium, 1935, 30; 1936, 57. Emil Frankel, Director of Division of Statistics and Research, Department of Institutions and Agencies, New Jersey, cited in Interstate Commission on Crime, *Handbook*, 1938, 131; Millspaugh, *Crime Control*, 274.

11
Denver Post, 10 January 1937, sec. 1.

12
Anslinger to C. H. Schoeffel, Acting Deputy Superintendent, New Jersey State Police, 22 December 1936, File 1960–9, NARA; untitled form submitted for 1936 by Colorado, compiled into "Seizures of Cannabis (Marihuana) in the United States, Calendar Year 1936, as Reported by State and Municipal Enforcement Officers," File 0480–36, NARA; Clair T. Sippel, Secretary, Legislative Reference Office, to Anslinger, 31 March 1937; Charles H. Querry, Director, Legislative Reference Office, to Will S. Wood, Acting Commissioner, Bureau of Narcotics, 26 January 1938, File 1960–9, NARA.

13
Anslinger and Oursler, *Murderers*, 38.

14
Kenneth Clark to Anslinger, 6 March 1935; Alfa F. Ostrander to Clark, 2 March 1935, File 1960–9, NARA; Kenneth Clark, "Murders Due to Marihuana Sweeping U.S.," *Denver Post*, 24 February 1935, sec. 3.

15
Anslinger and Cooper, "Marijuana: Assassin of Youth," *American Magazine* (July 1937), 18–19, 150ff; transcript of Anslinger broadcast, *Literary Digest*, 1 January 1938.

16
New York Times, August 1937; *Denver Post*, 8 August 1937. Merrill, *Marihuana*, 26.

17
Rocky Mountain News, 21 March 1936; Alamosa (Colorado) Rotary Club to J. Edgar Hoover, 25 January 1937; Hoover to Anslinger, 10 February 1937; Anslinger to F. G. Burns, Secretary, Alamosa Junior Chamber of Commerce, 17 February 1937, File 0480–36, NARA.

18
Colorado, *Session Laws*, 1937, ch. 139, 522; Colorado, *House Journal*, 32nd sess., 1937, entries for HB 364; Harry D. Smith to Anslinger, 5 May 1937, File 1960–9, NARA.

19
Smith to Anslinger, 5 May 1937; Will S. Wood to Smith, 13 May 1937; Smith to Anslinger, 21 May 1937, File 1960–9, NARA.

20
Denver Post, 2 May 1937, 6 August 1937.

21
Rocky Mountain News, 8 August 1937, 9 August 1937, 13 August 1937, 17 August 1937; *Denver Post*, 10 August 1937, 14 August 1937.

22
Rocky Mountain News, 2 September 1937; *Denver Post*, 1 September 1937, 10 September 1937.

23
Denver Post, 8 October 1937.

24
Colorado, Board of Health, *Biennial Report*, 1938–39, 9, 26–27.

25
Roy L. Cleere to Elizabeth Bass, 23 August 1940; Bass to Cleere, 9 September 1940; Anslinger to Bass, 14 September 1940; Bass to Anslinger, 16 September 1940, File 1960–9, NARA.

26
Interstate Commission on Crime, *Handbook*, 1938, "Report of the Narcotics Section to the General Session," 109. Will S. Wood to Thomas Lane, draft, 1938, File 0480–36, NARA.

27
Anslinger to V. L. Wood, 7 April 1938; correspondence of Rev. Devine and Anslinger from Devine to Anslinger, 9 February 1937, to Anslinger to Devine, 7 February 1939, File 0480–36, NARA; Anslinger, "Marihuana: The Assassin of the Human Mind," *Law Enforcement* (Missouri Peace Officers Association), 1 October 1941.

28
Rocky Mountain News, 6 December 1937; *Denver Post*, 18 August 1940, sec. 4, 12 January 1941, sec. 1; *Rocky Mountain News*, 10 March 1943.

29
Denver, Police Department, *Annual Report*, 1937, 62–64; 1938, 72–73; 1939, 88–90; 1940, 73–75; 1941, 57–60; 1942, 60–63; 1943, 59–62; 1944, 54–57; 1945, 52–55. James S. Henderson to Anslinger, 27 December 1944, enclosing Colorado district attorneys' reports on marijuana, File 1960–9, NARA.

Chapter 6: Creating the Modern Drug Dilemma

1
Traffic in Opium, 1947, 14; 1949, 12.

2
Colorado, Board of Health, *Report*, 1940–45, 98; 1946–47, 8–9.

3
A. B. Crisler to Anslinger, 13 January 1947, File 1960–9, NARA. Colorado, *Session Laws*, 1947, ch. 179, 400–401; Colorado, *Senate Journal*, 37th sess., 1947, entries for SB 181.

4
Crisler to James J. Biggins, 30 July 1947; Crisler to Anslinger, 11 April 1947, File 1960–9, NARA.

5
Crisler to Anslinger, 30 July 1947; Biggins to Anslinger, 5 August 1947, File 1960–9, NARA.

6
Terry A. Talent to Anslinger, 7 February 1949, File 1960–9, NARA. *Denver Post*, 7 February 1949 (editorial). Colorado, *Session Laws*, 1949, ch. 150, 353–55; Colorado, *Senate Journal*, 38th sess., 1949, entries for SB 281.

7
Traffic in Opium, 1949, 6–7.

8
Alan S. Meyer, ed., *Social and Psychological Factors in Opiate Addiction: A Review of Research Findings Together with an Annotated Bibliography* (New York, 1952), 60, 64, 2.

9
J. D. Reichard, "Some Myths about Marihuana," *Federal Probation* 10, no.

4; New York Mayor's Committee on Marihuana, *The Marihuana Problem in the City of New York* (Lancaster, Pa., 1944); Anslinger and Oursler, *Murderers*, 41–42.

10
Resolution of the National Convention of the National WCTU at Denver, September 1950, cited in *Traffic in Opium*, 1950, 30; WCTU, "The 'Dope' on Dope," "Marihuana, the New Dangerous Drug," "What We Should Know about Marihuana," "Leaf of Marihuana," "Criminal and Psychiatric Aspects Associated with Marihuana," *The Union Signal* (Evanston, Ill.), 1950.

11
Traffic in Opium, 1951, 9; 1952, 9; Herbert Brean, "A Short and Horrible Life," *Life*, 11 June 1951; Anslinger, "The Facts About Teenage Drug Addicts," *Reader's Digest*, October 1951, 83, cited in *Traffic in Opium*, 1951, 9; "Living Death: The Truth about Drug Addiction," File 1960–9, NARA.

12
Rocky Mountain News, 23 October 1950.

13
Anslinger to Senate Crime Investigation Committee, 28 June 1950, File 1960–9, NARA; *Traffic in Opium*, 1950, 8–10.

14
Denver Post, 14 July 1951.

15
Boggs Act, 65 Stat. 767, 1951; *Traffic in Opium*, 1937–53, p. 1 in all.

16
Traffic in Opium, 1951, 5; 1952, 12.

17
Ibid., 1950, 6; 1951, 9; 1952, 7; Colorado, *Session Laws*, 1945, ch. 118, 318.

18
Rocky Mountain News, 5 February 1951; Brean, "Short and Horrible Life," 121–23; *Rocky Mountain News*, 23 October 1950; *Denver Post*, 1 June 1951; HB 496; Talent to Anslinger, 14 December 1951; Anslinger to Talent, 20 December 1951, File 1960–9, NARA.

19
Denver Post, 5 July 1951; *Rocky Mountain News*, 2 July 1951, 18 May 1951, 22 May 1951.

20
Colorado WCTU, *Messenger*, April 1951; *Rocky Mountain News*, 21 December 1950; *Messenger*, October 1951.

21
Ralph W. Burns to Senator Edwin C. Johnson, 10 December 1951; G. W. Cunningham, Acting Commissioner of Narcotics, to Johnson, 7 January 1952, File 1960–9, NARA; *Traffic in Opium*, 1951, 9.

22
Denver Post, 10 July 1951, 29 July 1951.

23
Ibid., 4 January 1952; Talent to Anslinger, 16 January 1952, File 1960–9, NARA.

24
John W. Marsh to Anslinger, 12 February 1952, File 1960–9, NARA; Colorado, SB 20, 40th sess., 1952, 1st print; Colorado, *Session Laws*, 1952, ch. 39, 106–7; Talent to Anslinger,

26 February 1952, File 1960–9; *Rocky Mountain News*, 19 February 1952.

25
Denver Post, 1 June 1952.

26
Traffic in Opium, 1945–52, passim; Colorado, Board of Health, *Report 1952–53*, 39; Denver, Police Department, *Annual Report*, 1933, 48–49; 1934, 48–50; 1935, 59–61; 1936, 58–60; 1937, 62–64; 1938, 72–73; 1939, 88–90; 1940, 73–75; 1941, 57–60; 1942, 60–63; 1943, 59–62; 1944, 54–57; 1945, 52–55; 1946, 55–59; 1947, 56–58; 1948, 57–59; 1949, 57–61; 1950, 52–59; 1951, 25–27; 1952, 31–33.

27
Denver, Police Department, *Annual Report*, 1945, 52–55; 1952, 31–33.

28
Narcotic Control Act, 70 Stat., 567–75, 1956.

29
George O. Weber to Anslinger, 12 Sep-

tember 1956; G. W. Cunningham to Weber, 21 September 1956, File 1960–9, NARA.

30
Denver Post, 7 February 1957; Colorado, *Session Laws*, 1957, Narcotic Drugs, ch. 131, 352–54.

31
B. T. Mitchell to Anslinger, 19 February 1959, File 1960–9, NARA. Colorado, *Session Laws*, 1959, Narcotic Drugs, ch. 108, 388–91.

32
Colorado, *Session Laws*, 1953, chs. 93, 94, 95, 96, 257–65; 1955, chs. 128, 129, 296ff; Colorado, Board of Health, *Biennial Report*, 1954–55, 27.

33
Colorado, *Session Laws*, 1963, ch. 114, 345–6; for a general summary of this reorientation see Musto, *American Disease*, ch. 10.

34
Rocky Mountain News, 30 December 1963.

Courtesy Denver Public Library, Western History Department.

Index

References to illustrations are shown in italics.

75-88; post-war campaign by, 89-
97; and the Uniform Narcotic
Drug Act, 67-77. *See also*
Anslinger, Harry J.
Bureau of Prohibition, 58, 59
Burke, Carle W., 53

Caldwell, Samuel R., 85
Callen, Richard C., 54
Cannabis. *See Cannabis indica*;
Cannabis sativa; Marijuana
Cannabis indica, 10, 22, 34, 36, 52,
55
Cannabis sativa, 36, 52
Canon City (Colorado), 46, 54
Capitol Hill (Denver), 28-29, 34
Carbolic acid, 21
Carlson, George A., 32
Carlson, William A., 91
Catterson, A. D., 83
Celery Kola, 7
Central City Register, 3
Childers, T. E., 71
China, opium trade with, 2
Chinese, 30; and Denver's raid on
Chinatown, 4; laborers, 2; and
opium use, 2-5, 8, 14-15, 23, 26,
42
Chloral hydrate, 1, 5, 8-9, 10, 22,
24, 34, 36, 37, 38
Chlorine, 11
Chloroform, 1, 5-6, 22
Cholera, 27
Christian Science Monitor, 63
Clark, Ken, 80
Cleere, Roy L., 66, 70, 83
Coca-Cola, 7
Cocaine, 1, 6-7, 9, 13, 26-27, 47, 89,
103; addiction to, 12-13, 15, 20,
26, 28, 33, 92; and Denver's "dope
trust," 34; and the Harrison Act,
30, 33, 52, 55; is regulated in
Colorado, 13-14, 15, 22, 25-26,
31-34; is regulated in Denver, 14-
16, 19-22, 26-27, 48; Taft assesses Americans' use of, 24

Codeine, 10, 90
Colorado Act of 1952, 99-101
Colorado City (Colorado), 15
Colorado Insane Asylum, 12-13, 16,
45, 65
Colorado legislature, 12, 45, 55;
allows prohibition, 23; considers
marijuana legislation, 82-83;
considers narcotics legislation,
90-92, 97-98, 100, 101, 103;
revises poison and drug control,
21-22; views cocaine as a menace,
25
Colorado Medicine, 11
Colorado Pharmacal Association, 20,
31-32, 60, 70, 90-91
Colorado Psychopathic Hospital, 46,
65
Colorado Pure Food and Drug Act,
21, 25
Colorado Springs (Colorado), 11, 15,
20, 49, 95
Colorado State Board of Health, 15,
22, 28, 32, 45, 90, 102; aids in
marijuana control, 73, 77, 83-86.
See also Cleere, Roy L.
Colorado State Crime Commission,
97-98
Colorado State Hospital, 45. *See
also* Colorado Insane Asylum
Colorado State Medical Society, 21,
31-32, 41, 46, 90
Colorado State Teachers College, 80
Colorado Territory, vii, 1-5
Commission on Uniform State Laws,
55, 59, 68
Committee on Indian and Military
Affairs, 52
Committee on Medical Affairs, 52
Conference of State and Provincial
Health Officials, 77
Cooper, Courtney Ryley, 81
Cordials, 6-8
Costilla County (Colorado), 52, 82
Creel, George, 27
Cripple Creek (Colorado), 12, 20

Crisler, A. B., 90-91
Crowley, Clem, 35
Cures, 10-13, 17, 25, 27, 29, 41, 49.
  See also Opium; Patent medicines

Demerol, 90-91
Denver (Colorado), 17, 19, 34-35, 59, 82; anti-Chinese riot in, 4, 14; care of addicts in, 11, 33-34; drug use in, 8, 42, 64-66, 70-71, 87-88, 95-102; drug use by society, 14, 28-29, 34, 49; enacts ordinances, 2, 10, 14, 21, 26-27, 47-48. *See also* Bureau of Narcotics, Denver division of; Opium dens
Denver County (Colorado), 52
Denver Junior Chamber of Commerce, 97
Denver News, 81, 83-84
Denver Pharmaceutical Association, 15
Denver Post, 19, 35-36, *40*, 49, 50, *51*, 53, 69-71, 79, 83, 91, 94, 96, 98
Denver Times, 14, 20, 35, 42, 48
Denver Tribune, 3
Denver Women's Club, 35, 48, 101
Digitalis, 65
Dingley, A. G., 42-43, 44
Divers, Frank R., 82-83
Doctors. *See* Physicians
Dr. Haines' Golden Specific, 11
Dr. Pettey's Retreats, 11

Elixirs, 6-8, 29
Enteric fever, 17
Ergot, 65
Ether, 1, 6

Fairplay (Colorado), 5
Federal Bureau of Investigation (FBI), 77-78
Forest Retreat, 11

Garfield, James, 3
Georgetown (Colorado), 5

Glenwood Springs (Colorado), 11
Glycerine, 10
Godfrey's Cordial, 6
Gonzales, Pedro A., 52
Grand Junction (Colorado), 44, 54

Haralson, M. F., 73
Harding, Warren G., 44
Harrison Anti-Narcotic Act, 30-34, 49, 92, 103-04; effect of, on drug regulation, 38-39, 52, 58-59, 66, 68, 75-76, 78, 86; efforts to include cannabis in, 37-38, 54-55; implementation of, 41-42; leads to comprehensive Colorado act, 31-33; preempts Colorado laws, 43-44; regulates medical practice, 38, 44
Hashish, 25, 37, 52, 79, 90. *See also* Marijuana
Hayes, Oscar, 27
Hemp. *See* Marijuana
Heroin: addiction to, 28, 92; and Denver's "dope trust," 34; is regulated in Colorado, 22; postwar traffic in, 89-90, 96
Hispanics, and marijuana, 36-39, 41, 47-48, 52-54, 63-66, 82
Hop Alley. *See* Opium dens
Huerfano County (Colorado), 52
Hyoscine, 12
Hypnotics, 6, 24, 101, 103

Immigration Restriction Act of 1922, 53
Indians, and peyote, 34-36, 41, 46-47
Influenza, 17
Interstate Commission on Crime, 76, 86
Iodine, 11
Isonipecaine (Demerol), 90-91

James, Charles B., 27
Jimpson weed, 10
Jin Fuey Moy. *See* U.S. v. Jin Fuey Moy

Johnson, Edwin C., 70, 72, 73
Johnson, George S., 46
Jones-Miller Act. *See* Narcotic Drug
   Import and Export Act of 1922
Keeley Institute, 11
Kiowa Tribe, 34
Knous, W. Lee, 91
Knowles, Edwin K., 24-25
Koka-Nola, 7
Kolb, Lawrence, 46
Ku Klux Klan, 47, 53, 54

La Plata County (Colorado), 14
LaMoure, Superintendent (of
   Colorado State Hospital), 45
Larimer County (Colorado), 64
Larimer Street (Denver), 7
Las Animas County (Colorado), 36
Laudanum, 1, 6, 9, 20, 21
Leadville (Colorado), 3
Lear, Walter, 83
Love, John, 102
Lucero, Andres, 36, 38
Ludlow, Fitz Hugh, 37
Ludlow Massacre, 26

Manning, Joseph A., 65-67, 70-74
Mapeline, 65
Marijuana, 22, 37-38, 90, 103; and
   the Bureau of Narcotics, 57-81,
   92-97; is regulated in Colorado,
   36-39, 46, 52-54, 59, 61-62, 75,
   77, 79, 82-88, 104; is regulated in
   Denver, 47-48, 64-66; is regulated
   in the United States, 37-38, 54-
   55, 57-88. *See also Cannabis
   indica*; *Cannabis sativa*; Harrison
   Anti-Narcotic Act; Hashish;
   Marijuana Tax Act; Uniform
   Narcotic Drug Act
Marijuana Tax Act (MTA), 75-88,
   92-93
Market Street (Denver), 19, 22-23,
   27
McNichols, Stephen L. R., 97
Mercury, 10-11

Merrill, Frederick T., 81
Mexican Americans, Mexicans. *See*
   Hispanics
Milliken, Carl S., 64
Miners, mining camps, 1, 2, 13-14,
   26
Ministerial Alliance, 35
Model Anti-Narcotic Law of 1903,
   21, 25
"Morely Letter," 3
Morgan County (Colorado), 64
Morphine, 1, 9, 10, 27, 29, 47, 92;
   addiction to, 8, 12-13, 20, 28; in
   cures for addiction, 10; in patent
   medicines, 6, 25; is regulated in
   Colorado, 22, 90; is regulated in
   Denver, 14-16, 19-22; Taft
   assesses Americans' use of, 24
Mrs. Winslow's Soothing Syrup, 2
Munn's Elixir, 8
Myles, Glenn, 91

Narcotic Control Act of 1956, 100-01
Narcotic Drug Import and Export
   Act of 1922 (Jones-Miller Act),
   57, 100
Narcotics Division, Bureau of
   Internal Revenue. *See* Bureau of
   Internal Revenue
Narcotics Division, U.S. Department
   of the Treasury. *See* U.S. Depart-
   ment of the Treasury
National Association of Retail
   Druggists, 70
National Mother's Congress, 35
New Deal. *See* Roosevelt, Franklin
   D.
New York Academy of Medicine, 92-
   93
New York Times, 81
Nicotine. *See* Tobacco
Nutt, Levi G., 54-55, 57-58

O'Neill, Isabelle A., 69-70
Opiates. *See* Opium
Opium, vii, 1-17, 37, 53, 103; addic-

NATIONAL UNIVERSITY LIBRARY SAN DIEGO